CW00675021

Life on the Heath

Life on the Heath

The Making of a Cardiff Suburb

Gareth Williams

MERTON PRIORY PRESS

First published 2001

Published by
Merton Priory Press Ltd
67 Merthyr Road, Whitchurch
Cardiff CF14 1DD

© Gareth Williams 2001

ISBN 1 898937 30 3

Printed by
Dinefwr Press
Rawlings Road, Llandybie
Camarthenshire SA18 3YD

Contents

List of Tables

List of Illustrations

Picture Credits

1 South Wales Record Society; 2, 6 National Library of Wales; 3, 11, 12, 15 Glamorgan Record Office; 4, 5, 28, 29 National Museums and Galleries of Wales; 8 Cardiff Castle Collection; 13, 32, 41 Mrs Marjorie Beavis; 16 Cardiff Central Library; 18, 20, 30 Stewart Williams; 19 Ken Nunn Collection; 21, 24, 25 Mrs Doreen Ricketts; 22, 33 Arthur Turner; 27 Simmons Aerofilms; 31 British Oyxgen Co. Ltd; 34 National Assembly for Wales; 35, 36, 38, 42, 43 Western Mail & Echo; 40 Dr Eleunis Goodfellow.

Preface

This short book seeks to present an account of a Cardiff suburb which, although never a parish in its own right, has a distinctive and interesting history.

In my capacity as a Neighbourhood Watch Co-ordinator in the Heath I tried to identify common interests which would serve to draw branch members closer in order to increase our social cohesion and awareness. It occurred to me that the experience we all held in common as neighbours was that we lived in the same locality. I began gathering material which would portray our suburb in as interesting and varied a way as I could manage and, one Saturday in September 1996, I assembled a combination of maps, diagrams, photographs and snippets of information about the Heath in my garage and invited anyone who was interested to view them. The *South Wales Echo* provided first-rate publicity and about two hundred people attended. This response was far greater than I had expected. Visitors displayed an active interest; many provided further information and some suggested that the material on display might serve as the basis of a publication, which I have now attempted.

I am grateful to the staffs of Cardiff Central Library, the Glamorgan Record Office, the National Library of Wales, the National Museum of Wales and the Royal Commission on the Ancient and Historical Monuments of Wales for information and advice and their permission to reproduce material held by them. Information has also been gleaned from many local residents, to whom I extend my gratitude.

The Heath   Gareth Williams
Cardiff   September 2001

1 Cardiff and its environs, from George Yates's map of Glamorgan of 1799, showing the Heath to the north of the built-up area near the road to Caerphilly.

PART ONE

THE HEATH BEFORE 1800

The Heath: a Short Guide

During the second half of the twentieth century 'The Heath' is a name which has become familiar to people throughout much of Wales, since it is now largely synonymous with the modern University Hospital of Wales located in northern Cardiff. It appears as the complex of large buildings on the right-hand side of the picture on the cover of this book, an aerial photograph of the Heath from the west. The hospital takes its colloquial name from the suburb in which it was built in 1971. This suburb is broadly defined as the district which lies east of Caerphilly Road (seen crossing from right to left across the middle of the picture) as far as the Cardiff to Rhymney railway (seen crossing the background of the photograph), and extending north from Whitchurch Road as far as the Cardiff to Coryton railway. It is roughly oblong in shape and about a square mile in extent.

The original Heath, however, extended far beyond these limits. Before the early nineteenth century it was a great expanse of unfenced and uncultivated pasture land, left unenclosed as adjoining communities gradually cleared land closer to their settlements for cultivation, and valued by villagers as a source of rough grazing for their animals, wood for fuel and building, and an open space for recreation.

The Heath would have been familiar from early times to travellers, for it is crossed by an ancient routeway skirting the South Wales coastline which probably forded the River Taff near its tidal limit at Gabalfa. This route may have been adopted by the Romans in the first century A.D., when they built a military road intended to link the legionary fortress at Caerleon with a succession of forts along the South Wales coast. As it approached Cardiff this highway may have divided at a junction near the present-day village of Michaelstone-y-fedw. The main branch turned south-west, through St Mellons and Roath, to the fort near the estuary of the Taff, on the site of Cardiff Castle, before crossing the river nearby and continuing through Canton and Ely. The other branch may have by-passed the fort at Cardiff by following an older routeway across the Heath on the line of present-day Rhyd-y-pennau Road and Heathwood Road and across the ford at Gabalfa before rejoining the other road at Ely. At the present-day Birchgrove Crossroads it would have intersected another, well-attested, Roman road linking the forts at Cardiff and Brecon which ran north, roughly following the line of North Road and Caerphilly Road to Thornhill, continuing over Caerphilly Common and Gelligaer Common towards the Brecon Beacons. It must be admitted, however, that no archaeological evidence has ever been found to confirm that the route across the Heath was used in the Roman period. The Roman road from Cardiff to the north remained in use in Norman times, when it linked the castles at

Cardiff and Caerphilly.

Under the Normans Wales was divided into parishes and most of the Heath was incorporated within the parish of Llanishen. Its south-western corner, however, fell into that part of the parish of Llandaff which lay on the east bank of the Taff, opposite what became in the eleventh century the seat of the bishop of the new diocese of Llandaff. This remained the position until the late nineteenth century when this area became the new parish of Gabalfa after petitioning by local residents. The south-eastern corner of the Heath, roughly within a half-mile radius of the Heath Hotel, lay within the Cardiff parish of St John's, while a fringe of land on the west of the Heath lay within Whitchurch parish. Old Ordnance Survey maps show an inscribed stone on the boundary between Llanishen and Whitchurch where it crossed Caerphilly Road (near No 278). No trace of this stone now remains, which was probably removed when the road was widened in the early 1930s.

This huge area of open land on the outskirts of Cardiff became known as 'y Mynydd Bychan' ('the Great Heath') during medieval times. Rhys Meurig, in his *Antiquities of Glamorgan* (1578) lists many other commons in Glamorgan but none as extensive as the Great Heath, which stretched almost from the town walls of Cardiff as far as Cefn Onn and the line of hills which overlooked the town from the north. The Heath played a vital part in the local economy for it was claimed in common by the burgesses of Cardiff for grazing animals and cutting turf for fuel. Many people who lived in towns in the Middle Ages kept some animals and it was usual for them to claim areas of waste within easy distance of their homes as pasture for their geese, pigs, goats and cattle. These claims were jealously guarded. The right of the burgesses of Cardiff to graze animals on the Great Heath was confirmed in all the charters granted to the town from the early twelfth century. The charter of 1340, in addition to its customary confirmation of the burgesses' right to pasture and take turf, also gives them the right to keep a watchman to warn off others on the Great Heath and the Little Heath.

This became a matter for dispute in 1666, when the Cardiff manor court complained 'That the adjacent parishes of Roath, Llanishen, Whitchurch and other parishes do daily intrude on the said liberty and common pastures, for many years past, to the great wrong and detriment of the said Corporation'. The other side of the story appears in a survey of Roath Keynsham manor in 1702 where it was declared that the tenants of the manor had pasture rights on the Great Heath 'for all sorts of cattle'.[1] It is unclear how, if ever, these conflicting claims were resolved.

By the seventeenth century, however, changes in farming practice meant that the Heath began to lose its traditional role. It became neglected by the commoners and began to assume a wilder and more desolate aspect. Its surface was undulating, but featureless, except for the swamps in the undrained hollows and the groves of trees which were growing larger due to the commoners' failure to destroy young saplings.

[1] *Cardiff Records*, vol. ii.

It must have presented a bleak and daunting landscape to local folk as well as to strangers. Selecting a route through a bewildering maze of trails left by animals weaving around thickets, marshy hollows and other obstacles was the only option for anyone who was unfamiliar with it. Even locals may have avoided crossing it for no proper roads or bridges had been built on the Heath since Roman times.

A series of unpleasant incidents came to give the Heath a rather dismal reputation. During the closing years of the Civil War a violent skirmish resulting in much death and injury was fought there. Although their cause was already lost the Royalists made a short-lived local recovery and were besieging Cardiff Castle in February 1646. General Laugharne, commander of the Parliamentary army in Wales, abandoned his attack on Aberystwyth and marched his troops southwards in order to relieve Cardiff. As he was crossing the Heath he came across Sir Charles Kemeys leading a body of Royalists on their way to join the onslaught upon the castle. Heavy fighting broke out and nearly all the Royalists were killed or captured. Next morning General Laugharne's men attacked the main Royalist force outside the castle and defeated them. No doubt local folklore kept memories of this gruesome event alive for a long time, which may have been partly responsible for the Great Heath's unpleasant undertones.

This reputation lasted well into the eighteenth century. Was the cloth seal found recently on a Heath allotment (now in the National Museum of Wales) lost by a trader bewildered by his efforts to negotiate his way across the overgrown common? What dreadful tragedy lies behind this pitiful entry in St John's parish register in 1734: 'Sarah a child found on the Heath was buried'? The Heath must also have held bitter memories for the Lewis family of Llanishen: Gabriel Lewis, who was sheriff of Glamorgan in 1714–15, had three children, of whom Thomas, the eldest, was drowned in a pool on the Heath.

The Great Heath extended as an elongated tongue of empty land south of the Roath Brook almost as far as the hamlet of Roath itself. Here, it was called Waun Ddyfal or Little Heath and lay roughly in the vicinity of today's Crwys Road and Albany Road. For many centuries it had become the practice to hang criminals who had been condemned at Cardiff near the junction of the modern Crwys Road and City Road but tradition has it that some felons were also gibbeted on the Great Heath itself, probably alongside North Road. The records of the Great Sessions in Wales include indictments such as the following:

> Henry James, late of the parish of Eglwysilan, Catherine Griffith, otherwise known as Catherine James late of the parish of Saint Fagans, and Sarah Burt, otherwise known as Jenny Phillip, late of the parish of St Margarets, Birmingham, on the thirtieth day of August, 1791, about the twelfth hour of the night of the same day with force and arms feloniously and burglariously did break and enter the dwelling house of Catherine Price, widow, at Park and did steal, take and carry away a quantity of plate and wearing apparel to the value of £20.

These miscreants confessed to a catalogue of other crimes in addition, including breaking into a summer-house on the Great Heath owned by Thomas Edwards in 1790 and stealing china from it. They were found guilty by a grand jury at Cardiff on 3 September 1791. Sarah Burt was originally condemned to death but her sentence was commuted to transportation for life to New South Wales. Catherine Griffith was not so lucky for she was, reputedly, hanged on the Great Heath in October, 1791.

This particular story reappears in various forms. Another version places the theft in the 1840s and names the offender as Cati Goch (Kate the Redhead), a servant at Greenmeadow House, Tongwynlais, who was persuaded by a gipsy lad camped nearby to steal some silverware from her employers, the Lewis family (who were related to the Prices of the Parc). As soon as she was interrogated, she confessed and pleaded for clemency from the family, but she was tried and condemned to death. Tradition has it that she was brought from Cardiff to the Heath and hanged somewhere between Heath Turnpike Gate (which stood a short distance south of the point where the Roath Dock branch railway passed under North Road) and the junction of Caerphilly Road and Merthyr Road. Before dying she cursed Greenmeadow House and its occupants. Her ghost was supposed to have haunted the house until it was demolished in the 1940s. In reality, all hangings in Cardiff by the 1840s took place at the gaol.

Over the centuries, the Great Heath gradually shrank as encroachment took place, with parcels of land fenced off on its fringes. Some were taken by poor people desperately seeking to eke out a meagre livelihood from a tiny plot of land. Larger plots were appropriated by farmers or landowners. A court baron held at Cardiff in 1666 complained thus:

> And they say that the said Town [i.e. Cardiff] hath received great wrong and injury by Thomas Lewis, late of Llanishen, Esquire, deceased, who in his life inclosed by estimation 60 acres of land or thereabouts, scituate upon the Said Great Heath, which said Thomas Lewis in regard the said Corporation was not nor is not able to show any title for the same ... And by reason of this and several other encroachments and building of several cottages on the said Heath, the said Town and Corporation will be utterly disfranchised of their priviledges and liberties ...[1]

According to one local historian, D.L. George, gypsy squatters tried to settle on the Great Heath in the seventeenth century but were driven away by local opposition. Some local squatters on the Heath are mentioned as recently as the end of the eighteenth century.[2]

Part of Roath manor is shown on a Bute estate map of about 1775 (Plate 2) which shows the Nant Fawr flowing southwards through the area now occupied by Roath

---

[1] *Cardiff Records*, ii.
[2] Letter to the *South Wales Echo*, 7 Feb. 1955.

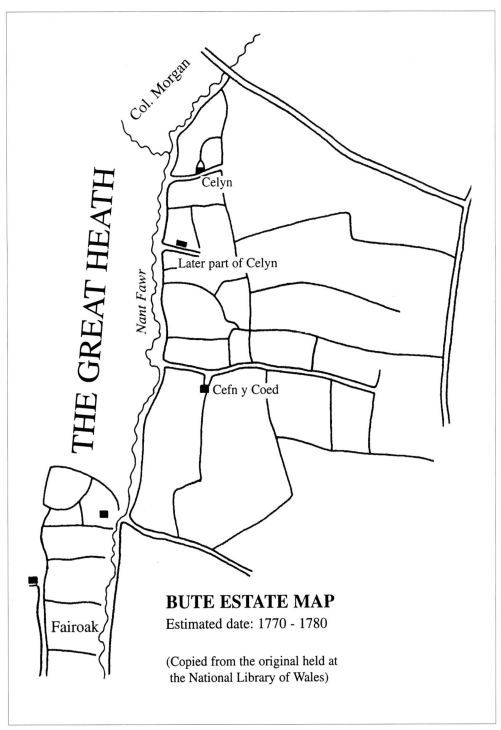

BUTE ESTATE MAP

Estimated date: 1770 - 1780

(Copied from the original held at
the National Library of Wales)

2 An extract from a plan of the manor of Roath, part of the Bute Estate, of about 1775, showing the Nant Fawr flowing through the area now occupied by Roath Lake.

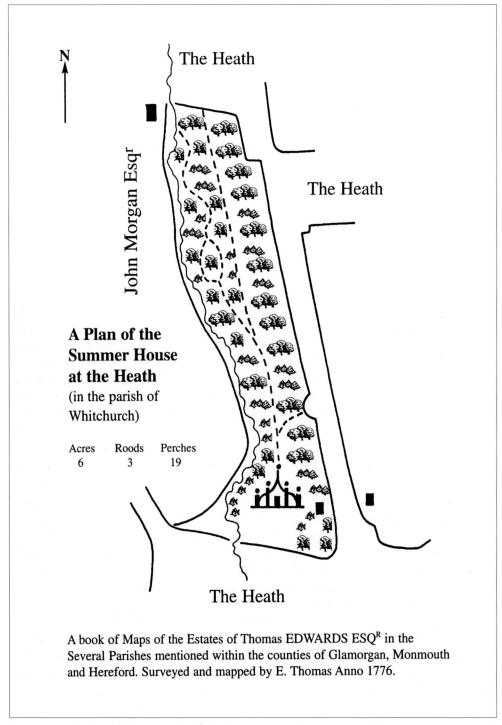

N

The Heath

John Morgan Esqr

The Heath

A Plan of the Summer House at the Heath
(in the parish of Whitchurch)

Acres	Roods	Perches
6	3	19

The Heath

A book of Maps of the Estates of Thomas EDWARDS ESQ^R in the Several Parishes mentioned within the counties of Glamorgan, Monmouth and Hereford. Surveyed and mapped by E. Thomas Anno 1776.

3 'A Plan of the Summer House at the Heath', from a survey of the estates of Thomas Edwards, made in 1776.

Park Lake. The fields of Celyn and Cefn y Coed farms now lie under the modern Lakeside residential developments, whereas the map shows the Great Heath extending east as far as the brook which formerly flowed down the valley now occupied by the lake. Another map (Plate 3), drawn by Edward Thomas within a few years of the Bute map, shows how the western fringe of the Great Heath lay well within the parish of Whitchurch during the mid eighteenth century. It also shows a summer-house which the Edwards family owned on the edge of the Heath.

Since the beginning of the nineteenth century, the Heath has experienced a greater transformation than at any time during the previous thousand years. That story is outlined in the second half of this study: the remainder of this first chapter considers other aspects of the Heath's history before the Industrial Revolution.

Axe and Arrow

Two ancient man-made implements lay buried in the ground of the Heath for thousands of years before coming to light during the mid twentieth century. The older object is a polished flint axe-head and the other is a delicate little flint arrow-head.

The axe-head (Plate 4), now in the Department of Archaeology of the National Museum of Wales, is about 4,500 years old. It was found in a garden in Waun Fawr Road which, although not strictly within the boundaries of the modern suburb, would have been well within the confines of the original Great Heath. The blade is about five inches long; its wooden handle has long since rotted away. Flint is an extremely tough stone and the fact that the axe-maker had managed to polish it shows that people had already grasped a difficult skill at that early stage of evolution. Soon, their mastery of a whole range of basic proficiencies would enable Stone Age people to overcome the limitations of their natural environment and control it for their own benefit. The Heath axe-head is made of flint which does not occur naturally in Wales; it must have been manufactured at some distant source and brought to the district by a trader.

The other discovery (Plate 5), a delicate little arrow-head now also in the National Museum, was made by a resident of The Crystals in the 1950s when he was digging his garden. He must have had sharp eyesight to spot it for it is barely an inch in dimension. Although made of flint about 4,000 years ago, it is certain that this arrow-head was not fabricated by a Stone Age man. Its style is more refined than arrow-heads of that era and it must have needed a greater degree of skill to shape its two tangs and saw edges. All its features point to the fact that it must have been made by a complete stranger to Wales, a newcomer belonging to a race of people who originated from the Mediterranean region that is present-day Spain. They were a very restless and vigorous folk who had uprooted themselves from their native environs and had migrated northward through Europe, possibly in the lee of warmer weather. They were noticeably different in appearance from the Stone Age inhabitants of Wales; they were stockier and their heads were rounder. H.N. Savory described them as 'robust,

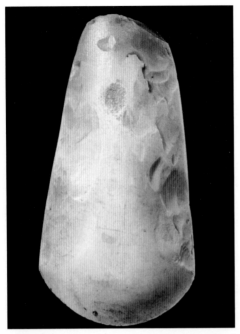

4 Stone Age axe-head found at Waun Fawr Road.

with broad skull, often flattened at the back and with rugged facial features'. Archaeologists call them Beaker Folk from their practice of placing artistically decorated pottery beakers in the graves of their dead, whom they buried in a crouching position.

How did the owner of the tiny arrow-head come to leave it behind on the Heath? Did he lose it? Was it stolen from him? Had he been fighting other people or had he been trading arrow-heads with them? Was he a shepherd guarding a flock of grazing animals? Was he on his own or with a group of kinsmen? If he was with a group were they merely passing by or did they stay long enough to build temporary huts? Sadly, none of these questions can be answered from the discovery of a single artefact.

Ffynnon Llandenis

Christianity first came to Wales with the conquering armies of the Roman Empire. The alleged third-century martyrdom of Saints Aaron and Julius near the legionary fortress of Isca at Caerleon indicates that evangelists were already trying to influence the local populace by that time. The new faith gained sufficient hold in the south-eastern corner of Wales to survive the collapse of Roman civilisation; Christian burials in the Vale of Glamorgan and a church built on the ruins of Caerwent Roman town indicate that Christianity maintained its significance during the years following the withdrawal of the Imperial armies to the Continent in A.D. 383.

It is certain that the faith did not spread directly to the remainder of Wales from its early origins in the south-east. This process began after large numbers of refugees fleeing from the attacks of the Pagans on the Continent landed in present-day Pembrokeshire in the fifth century. E.G. Bowen, in his book *Settlements of the Celtic Saints in Wales*, shows how they subsequently spread inland by following the former Roman roads eastwards across Wales. There were fervent Christians in their midst and some of them began the practice of building rough huts or 'cells' here and there along their routes where they would live the spartan life of hermits devoted to worship and the conversion of the local populace to the new faith. In some instances they would settle at a chosen destination but, more often than not, their zeal led them to move onward in search of fresh converts. In this way, they originated a process whereby the whole of Wales came to be covered by a network of early Christian settlements.

Their influence duly reached south-east Wales where it acted either to revive or strengthen the spiritual life of this early cradle of Christianity. By the fifth century the first three known Celtic missionaries began to evangelise in the Vale of Glamorgan and the Vale of Usk. They were Saints Dyfrig, Cadog and Illtud who travelled the old Roman roads to build on the work already achieved by greatly adding to the number of Christian settlements. Cadog and Illtud went on to establish monastic settlements at Llancarfan and Llantwit Major which became renowned centres of learning. Students taught there went on to perpetuate the faith in the manner of the early 'saints'.

5 Bronze Age arrow-head found at the Crystals.

It is traditionally believed that one of Illtud's pupils set up his own little 'cell' within a few hundred yards of the old road across the Heath, near the present-day Rhyd-y-pennau. The Latin form of his name is assumed to have been 'Dionysius', which might have been pronounced locally 'Nysan' or 'Isan'. Centuries later it might have evolved into 'Denys' when pronounced by the Norman French conquerors of Glamorgan. Dionysius is supposed to have located his cell near a spring, for he would depend on its water to perform holy sacraments such as baptism in addition to satisfying his normal domestic needs.

In the the seventh-century 'Life of Saint Samson' there is an account of St Illtud and his former pupil Isan:

> Illtyd was ill and failing when two abbots visited him, one named Isanus and the other Athoclus. The old man was glad to see them for he knew that he was about to die.
>
> 'At the third watch of the night', he said, 'I, in your presence, will be borne to heaven and you, brother Isanus, shall see angels with golden wings carry my soul away. Then, in fifteen days' time, you, Athoclus, will pass to your rest and Isanus shall see angels carry your soul away but they will have wings of lead because your love for the things of this world weigh you down. Due to your saintly life, however, God will purge your money-greed out of you. Then, in forty days, you, Isanus, will also pass to your rest.'

And, as the old man had foretold, so it came to be.

Saint Illtud is said to have died on 7 November but the precise year is not specified; historians speculate that it may have been around 530–540. If the 'Life of Saint Samson' is an accurate account it may be surmised that Saint Isan died on 16 December at about that time.

The Normans had conquered the low-lying coastal land of Glamorgan between the rivers Rhymney and Ogmore by the year 1100. Their leader, Robert Fitzhamon, presented his trusted followers with lands in the Vale of Glamorgan in return for their loyalty when the Welsh counter-attacked. Fitzhamon kept for himself a large slice of territory lying between Caerphilly Mountain and the sea, bounded on the west by the

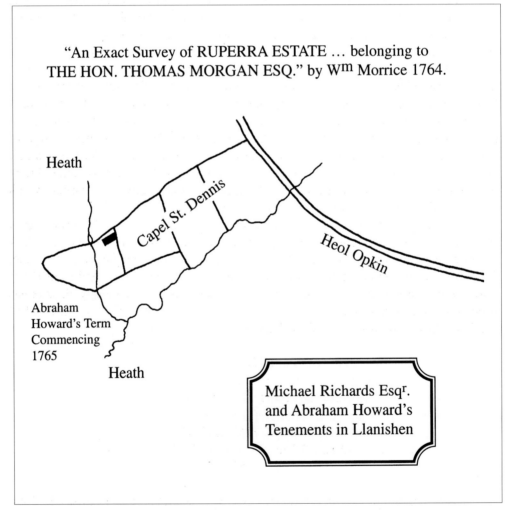

6 An extract from William Morrice's survey of Thomas Morgan's Ruperra Estate (1764), showing the site of Capel St Dennis.

river Taff and on the east by the river Rhymney. This coincided with the ancient Welsh administrative district (a commote) of Cibwr, which became the manor of Cardiff, centred on the former Welsh lord's castle there, which Fitzhamon rebuilt.

The Normans undertook a complete remodelling of religious life in Wales so that it would fit in with their new administrative pattern. They organised the network of churches originally set up by the saints into parishes, each served by a single church. Saint Isan's church on the Great Heath, along with others at Llanedeyrn, Llanforda and Roath, all lay within Cibwr, now the manor of Cardiff. Robert Fitzhamon made them all redundant when he formed a new parish whose limits coincided with those of the manor of Cardiff. He built a new parish church dedicated to Saint Mary in Cardiff.

Because St Mary's church lay near the southern boundary of its parish it became impracticable for people who lived in the northern and eastern extremities to travel such a distance to attend worship. Soon, the practice emerged of allowing parishioners who lived near the original Welsh churches to treat them as chapels-of-ease. This arrangement seemed to satisfy those living near Llanedeyrn, Llanforda and Roath to the east but discontent rumbled on amongst parishoners who lived in the north-east of the parish who still appeared to find travelling down to Saint Isan's church on the Great Heath cumbersome. Eventually the problem was resolved in the thirteenth century when the area served by the chapel-of-ease on the Great Heath was split in two. A new stone church dedicated to Saint Denys (the Norman French version of Dionysius) was built to the east to serve a new parish called Lisvane. The western half became the parish of Llanishen (i.e. the church of St Isan) and a new stone church was built in the fourteenth century about a mile north of Dionysius's chapel, which in 1180 had been granted to Tewkesbury Abbey.

Traditionally, it is believed that St Dionysius's oratory lay close to the spring which rises in the Oval Park between Rhyd-y-pennau Library and Cardiff High School. A Ruperra estate map of 1764 at the National Library of Wales (Plate 6) marks Capel St Dennis on the Great Heath at the confluence of Llanishen Brook and Nant Fawr. Early Ordnance Survey maps also place it in the same location. Recently, the site has been suitably denoted by the planting of a Hungarian Oak near the southern end of the footpath which crosses the Oval Park, with an accompanying plaque:

PLANTED BY
LLANISHEN
LOCAL HISTORY SOCIETY
NOVEMBER 1993
TO MARK THE SITE OF
LLANISHEN'S FIRST CHURCH
A.D. 535

J.H. Matthews, compiler of the renowned *Cardiff Records*, had this to say in 1898 about the spiritual context of the spring by Dionysius's chapel:

7 Fynnon Llandenis in 1999.

> It is known to old inhabitants as Ffynnon Llandenis ... and has for ages
> past been regarded with veneration by the country folk. This was owing
> to its association with the memory of a saint and to the reputation it
> enjoyed as a healing well. Its water was believed to possess singular
> curative properties especially in cases of rheumatism and scurvy and also
> for the eyes ... I have been informed by old people living hard by that
> down to recent times this well was resorted to for the cure of these com-
> plaints.

No doubt, these same old people were also familiar with a rather more sinister side
to Ffynnon Llandenis. It was said to be haunted by a ghost taking the form of a Ladi
Lwyd (Grey Lady) which could occasionally be seen wandering nearby, bemoaning
the fact that she was being punished for all the sins she had committed during her
lifetime. She was sure to appear to any drover who happened to visit the well and
would follow him as he continued his journey. Was the Ladi Lwyd running a
campaign to maintain the well's purity by trying to prevent cattle from fouling the
water?

A final quotation taken from M. Trevelyan's *Folk Lore and Folk Stories of Wales*
(1909) gives us a glimpse of activities that took place a century ago at another healing
well about four miles from Ffynnon Llandenis:

There is a tradition that Taff's Well was famous for its healing powers in Roman times … The well was reputed to cure rheumatism and lameness within one month of bathing there. A corrugated iron structure was erected over it to preserve the modesty of the bathers. When a man bathed it was customary to hang a pair of breeches outside to indicate the sex of the bather within; women hung up an essentially feminine garment … Visitors paid annual subscriptions to keep it in repair. During the nineteenth century young people assembled at Taff's Well on the eighth Sunday after Easter, dipped their hands in the well and scattered drops of water over one another before moving away to the nearest green space to spend the remainder of the day in dancing and merriment.

Taff's Well built up a reputation as a health resort during the nineteenth century. Conceivably, Ffynnon Llandenis might have developed a similar role.

The Battle of the Great Heath

According to tradition, one of the most crucial episodes in the early history of South Wales occurred on the Great Heath in 1090. In that year it is said that the native Welsh of Glamorgan were overthrown by Norman invaders in a great battle there. Their prince, Iestyn ap Gwrgant, was forced to flee and the victorious Norman leader, Robert Fitzhamon, after claiming the area around Cardiff for himself, presented his twelve trusted knights with lands in the Vale of Glamorgan as a reward for their loyalty and support during the onslaught.

The battle itself was the culmination of a complicated sequence of events, which were described thus in 1896:[1]

> It is not before the eleventh century—the time of Iestyn ap Gwrgant—that we find a firm footing in tracing the history of Cardiff. The Normans were then in the land and from that time on the history of the town is closely associated with the Conqueror's followers. Glamorgan,—the Land of Morgan,— passed into the hands of strangers a decade or so before the end of the eleventh century. The change was the outcome of revenge and treachery.
>
> During the time Iestyn ruled in Glamorgan, as a tradition of considerable antiquity states, a feud existed between him and Rhys ap Tewdwr, the Lord of Dyfed, which was caused by the latter's attempt to possess himself of Iestyn's wife. Being the weaker chieftain, Iestyn dispatched a

[1] *Cardiff: an Illustrated Handbook* (ed. J.Ballinger) (1896).

messenger—Einon ap Collwyn—to apply for assistance against his neighbour and enemy promising him his well-dowered daughter in marriage if his mission proved successful. Einon went, and succeeded, and brought back with him a Norman Knight—Robert Fitzhamon—accompanied by twelve other knights, double that number of esquires and a force of three thousand men. The mercenaries, joined by Einon ap Collwyn's own soldiers, met the army of Rhys ap Tewdwr somewhere near Hirwaun, on the ridge between the sources of the Rivers Dare and Rhondda. A battle ensued, Rhys being defeated and slain and his head cut off.

When the battle was over Fitzhamon and his men were dismissed and were to have returned home from Penarth by sea. Einon ap Collwyn now applied for his part of the bargain, the hand of Nest. To the suitor's great disappointment and disgust, Iestyn refused to fulfil his promise. Einon forthwith hurried after Fitzhamon. Having related Iestyn's ingratitude he urged the Normans to smite him hip and thigh and possess themselves of his territory.

The advice was taken and Fitzhamon and Iestyn now met as enemies on the Heath, just where lies the northern boundary of the borough, a spot that has been the scene of more than one bloody engagement in the history of Cardiff. Victory favoured the Norman filibusters and after his defeat Iestyn fled to hide his disgrace in the quiet shades of Keynsham Abbey, where he died and was buried. Nest, his daughter, was handed over to Einon and Glamorgan was divided between the Norman knights, Fitzhamon taking the lion's share of the spoil, including Cardiff and its castle and a large slice of the surrounding countryside.

Most of this story, apart from the battle itself, can be traced back to a manuscript in Cardiff Central Library, entitled the 'Winning of the Lordship of Glamorgan out of the Welshmen's Hands', written in about 1565 by Sir Edward Stradling of St Donats Castle, near Llantwit Major. He was a well-educated man who had built up a library of valuable books and manuscripts at his home and who showed a deep interest in history and matters of culture. From the vague, confused and often conflicting information that he gathered from as wide a variety of sources as circumstances allowed in those days he made a sincere attempt to compile what he considered to be a balanced and rational chronicle of the Norman occupation of Glamorgan. But, can it withstand modern critical inspection?

Sadly, we must concede that this colourful account which, for over three hundred years, was widely accepted as a true record, is largely fictitious. Modern historians accept the evidence found in 'Brut y Tywysogion' ('Chronicles of the Princes') which states that the Lord Rhys ap Tewdwr was actually killed near Brecon in 1093 whilst fighting Norman invaders in that area. Neither Iestyn ap Gwrgant, nor Einon ap Collwyn, nor Robert Fitzhamon was involved in his death. The story about Fitzhamon and his Twelve Knights receiving land in Glamorgan in reward for helping Einon ap

Collwyn to overthrow Iestyn ap Gwrgant, his king, was probably concocted by the bards in an attempt to console their Welsh lords for their defeat at the hands of the Normans. It was easier to swallow a story that explained how the Normans had been invited into Glamorgan in the first instance and had gained land here purely as a result of fighting by the Welsh amongst themselves!

Stradling cannot be blamed for accepting a biased account of the initial Norman onslaught upon Glamorgan. During the sixteenth century, historical enquiry had not yet developed a modern critical approach. He probably did his best to select what appeared to be the most plausible version of past events. It was true that Robert Fitzhamon had conquered a fringe of land, no wider than five miles, along the Severn shoreline between the rivers Rhymney and Ogmore sometime during the 1090s. It may also have been true that he had given some of his friends land there in order to secure their contining support.

Stradling names the following Twelve Knights and the manors given them:

Robert de St Quentin	Llanbleddian
Gilbert de Humphreville	Penmark
Peter le Sor	Peterston
William de Londres	Ogmore
Roger Berkrolles	East Orchard
Richard de Granville	Neath
Pagan de Turberville	Coity
Reginald de Sully	Sully
John Fleming	St Georges
Oliver St John	Fonmon
Richard Syward	Talyfan
William le Esterling	St Donats

Modern writers, beginning with G.T. Clark, have shown that nine of these can be totally discounted for a combination of two reasons: first, the manors of Llanbleddian, Neath, Coity and Talyfan were completely beyond the territory conquered by Fitzhamon, and second, the Berkrolles, Granville, Turberville, Sully, Fleming, St John, Syward and Esterling families came to live in Glamorgan after Fitzhamon's death in 1106. The le Esterling family is particularly interesting because they were not even a Norman family but had originated from present-day Switzerland. The first member of their family to live at St Donats was Sir Peter de Strätlinges who acquired the estate as the result of his marriage to Joan, heiress of the de Howey family, at the end of the thirteenth century.

Significantly, however, Stradling asserted that he was a descendant of the le Esterling family. He claimed that Sir William le Esterling was one of the Twelve Knights who fought with Fitzhamon in 1090 and was rewarded with the manor of St Donats for his loyalty. This was a deliberate falsehood for he had already drawn up a detailed family tree which showed that his family could not be traced back further than the end of the thirteenth century in Glamorgan. So, he set about adding seven fictitious generations to link Sir Peter de Strätlinges with an alleged 'Sir William le Esterling' who fought for Robert Fitzhamon.

What was the motive behind Stradling's deceit? He probably saw an opportunity to promote his family's prospects, not only within Glamorgan but also more widely. He knew that the descendants of all the first Norman families to settle in Glamorgan had either died out or moved away and he realised that he was free to promote the fabrication that the Stradlings of St Donats were the only family still living on an estate which had been granted to them by Robert Fitzhamon himself. Obviously, this assertion gave the Stradlings a unique social and political standing.

What about the Battle of the Great Heath? May we continue to believe that it actually occurred? Why not? We know that Iestyn ap Gwrgant had been overthrown by Robert Fitzhamon during his attack upon Glamorgan at the end of the eleventh century. Some historians speculate that Iestyn might easily have lived on the fringe of the Great Heath at Llystalybont, the mansion of the original Welsh 'maenor' at Cardiff. Besides that, the Heath was as good a place as any to meet an enemy—dry, level, and free from cultivated ground and woodland. Stradling may have been correct in locating the site of the fatal battle even though the remainder of his account was fanciful!

Racing on the Heath

In the mid eighteenth century Cardiff Corporation, aided by certain local gentry, introduced the fashionable sport of horse-racing to Glamorgan. The Great Heath was an ideal location for a racecourse for Cardiff: it was an open expanse of fairly level land which did not have to be bought or leased since it was held in common ownership by the burgesses and others. By the early 1760s a two-mile course, a rounded lozenge in plan, had been constructed, neatly straddling the old road across the Heath on a spur of land between the Wedal Brook on the west and Llanishen Brook on the east. Wedal Brook, better known today as Ton-yr-ywen Brook, runs down between Ton-yr-ywen Avenue and St Edwen Gardens, under Heathwood Road between Nos 55 and 57 (where the stone parapet above the culvert can be seen), across Heath Playing Fields and under the University Hospital into the Wedal Brook before finally joining Roath Brook. Llanishen Brook flows through The Crystals and under the Three Arches bridge to join Nant Fawr opposite Cardiff High School.

There was a stand and starting house at the main entrance to the course. In terms of the present-day landscape this starting point would lie near the gardens of Nos 45–51 on the west side of Heath Park Avenue. From here the course aimed southward along the line of King George V Drive East, before turning sharply west to run beneath the Heath Leisure Centre. It then began to veer northward, passing under the midway point of King George V Drive West, and the top ends of St Anthony Road

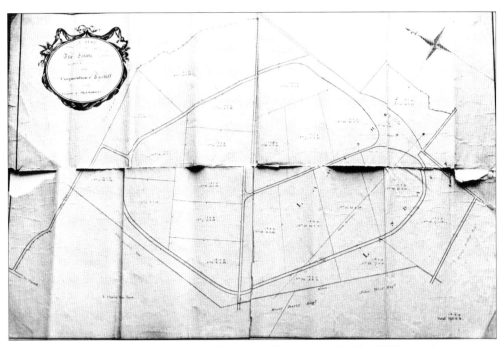

8 A map of 1805 showing the racecourse on land at the Heath owned by Cardiff Corporation.

and St Benedict Crescent, before turning directly northward to pass beneath Heathwood Road (under Nos 61–63). It continued north along the line of St Gowan Avenue and St Edwen Gardens, veering north-east under the top ends of Heathway and St Brioc Road, then sharply south eastward to run along the line of Maes-y-coed Road, crossing Crystal Wood Road beneath Nos 1–3 to follow the line of the footpath down to Heathwood Road. It passed beneath Heathwood Road at that point, continuing towards Heath Halt Low Level where it turned sharply south to run alongside Heath Halt Road to its junction with Heath Park Avenue, finally returning to the starting point on the west side of Heath Park Avenue. The edges of the course were fringed with a ditch and bank, some sections of which came to be lined with trees and bushes in time. All this area was, of course, open common land during the 1760s.

A race between an English-owned and a Welsh-owned horse is recorded as having been run at the Heath in 1764. The following year, two exciting races were run there on 2 September, first for a stake of £10 between the winning horse of Captain Mathew of Llandaff and that of Lewis Morgan of Whitchurch, and second for a stake of £50 between the horses of Edward David of Gelligaer and John Thomas of Llanwonno, which was won by the latter. In December 1766 the horses of Pengam and Llandaff Mill competed for a £10 stake. By 1790 racing at the Heath had become a properly organised and well-attended feature of the social life of Cardiff.

Plate 8 shows the racecourse straddling the old road across the Heath (Heathwood

Road today) with a starter's box, referred to as 'the Chair', at one of the main points of access on today's Heath Park Avenue. There was also direct access to the starting point by a lane from Heathwood Road.

Cardiff Corporation continued to make regular contributions to racing on the Heath; in 1784 they granted a sum of 10 guineas while from 1796 they paid an annual contribution of £5 5s. Subscriptions were also received from the Marquess of Bute on various occasions.

When the Great Heath was enclosed at the beginning of the nineteenth century the corporation kept the 150-acre site of the racecourse as part of their 330-acre share of the award under the 1801 Act. This was presumably done because they were anxious to retain the racecourse and ensure its upkeep. The corporation minutes for 1811 contain this entry:

> 10th June. Mr Wood and Mr Hollier took a conveyance of the Race Ground, subject to the Conditions that the Same should be thrown open for three successive weeks in each year, so long as the races shall continue to be held, on their having notice from the Steward or Clerk of the Course; and not to plough or break up the same for tillage.[1]

But the full sum was never paid to the corporation and they were forced to recover the land by an action at the 1819 Great Sessions.

The corporation kept up their support for the course in 1817 by paying 10 guineas towards the Town Plate, which would be awarded annually. By now, however, there were signs of a decline in racing and the corporation redoubled their efforts to revive it. In 1824, 'It being expedient to promote the interests of this town by furthering the subscription to the racing fund', they 'Resolved that the next year the sum of £20 be allowed towards a plate of £50 to be called the Town Plate, provided that there is a subscription made by the inhabitants of £30. Also resolved that a sum of £10 10s. 0d. be allowed by the Corporation towards the said racing fund'.

Despite these efforts a newspaper report of July 1825 gives an idea of the true situation:

> The races at Cardiff terminated on the 10th instant but we are sorry to say that the second day's proceedings were inferior to the first. The genteel company assembled on the raceground was greater than had been known for a number of years but a multitude of gazers will not ensure good racing. It is strange that in Glamorgan this noble sport, should of late years, have fallen off in the manner that it has done.

For the next twenty years racing at the Heath was spasmodic and only moderately

---

[1] *Cardiff Records*, iv.

successful. A newspaper report of 1840 gives a brief picture of the racecourse, together with a description of the countryside surrounding the line of the steeplechase from Greenmeadow mansion, Tongwynlais, to the racecourse stand itself. The first part, through Pentwyn and the Philog, passed through farmland criss-crossed by ditches and hedges with an occasional lane or brook whilst the last mile across the Heath lay through open land. The ditch and bank bordering the old racecourse were still intact for the horses had to jump them in order to gain access to the track. It is worth noting that, during an age when people had to pay for medical attention, the doctor had placed himself in a most strategic position on the course.

Tongwynlais to Heath Steeplechase

On Monday morning, March 16th, 1840, Cardiff Race Course presented a most animated and lively scene dotted with groups of spectators. It had been rumoured for some time that the Parc Hunt Club was to hold a Steeple Chase. The start would take place at the lawn of Greenmeadow House, Tongwynlais, and the winning point would be at the Stand of the Race Course. As early as 11.00 a.m. the roads from Cardiff and Llandaff to the Heath were full of pedestrians or people on horseback or in gigs … etc. As the mass of spectators increased it was noticed that there was a sprinkle of the elite of the neighbourhood of the area present along with officers of H.M. Hussars and Royal Artillery quartered at Cardiff and Newport.

At 2.45 p.m. the carriage from Greenmeadow drew up at the Stand bringing Mr and Mrs Lewis followed by other vehicles bringing their friends and visitors. By now the whole line of the chase, marked out with crimson flags, was skirted with anxious spectators among whom the glittering uniforms of the Hussars appeared. The distance from Greenmeadow to the Stand was three and a half miles over heavy, rough land, well fenced, with a brook and here and there a ditch. The line crossed the main road from Cardiff to Caerphilly and was intersected by several rough roads. Start took place promptly at 3.00 p.m. The horses were TARTAR (Mr Vaughan), SAM SLICK (Mr Bradley), PREMIER (Mr Henry Lewis) and FROLIC (Mr John Williams).

Sam Slick took the lead at the first fence, followed by Tartar and Premier. Sam Slick was again first at the second fence and Premier close behind. The four were abreast at Pentwyn lane which they all cleared in line and continued without check. When nearing Whitchurch, Tartar, Sam Slick and Frolic bore off to the right of the flags in order to gain a shorter leap over the brook but Premier kept close left and cleared it in excellent style. They next made the Philog lands where the fences were stronger. Here was a most terrific leap to counter, a very high bank and hedge and an awful looking ditch behind; this was considered to be the most critical spot on the line. Over the four horses flew, much to the astonishment of the doctor who had placed himself there, expecting trouble. Six minutes had elapsed and half the ground had been covered but the heaviest was to come in the form of difficult fences. The next leap was beautifully cleared by Sam Slick, Tartar and Premier but Frolic refused and this held her well back.

The Stand now appeared; the last mile being entirely open, with good, stiff fences to clear. The last fence but one was beautifully cleared by the first three horses abreast but Frolic again refused. The last fence which bounded the Race Course was no joke with a ditch hedged with thick gorse. Tartar was first over then Sam Slick and Premier. A general push was now made and Tartar won by two lengths in twelve and a half minutes. No accident whatever occurred even though the number of fences exceeded thirty.[1]

We can surmise that racing on the Heath had outlived its proper life by 1849, when the land on which the course lay was sold to Wyndham Lewis for £3,100. Formal meetings must have come to an end at that time, but occasional events sanctioned by the Lewis family persisted for some years, as this report shows:

the following races were held at the grounds of the Heath, the seat of the respected High Sheriff of Glamorgan, Wyndham William Lewis, Esq. They were run over part of the old Race Course. Cards were printed. About 1.00 p.m. North Road was crowded with sportsmen making their way towards the Heath on foot, on horseback or in vehicles. On the course we found a large concourse of sportsmen.[2]

Was this the final event to be held on the Heath Racecourse? Did people remember that it would celebrate its centenary in about five years' time? Did they mark the occasion somehow in 1860?

[1] *Cardiff and Merthyr Guardian*, 21 March 1840.
[2] Ibid., 7 April 1855.

PART TWO

THE HEATH SINCE 1800

The Enclosure of the Heath

At the opening of the nineteenth century a critical decision was made concerning the future of the Great Heath, which would change forever the distinctive aspects of the district which had characterised it for over a thousand years. It would cease to be a heath, except in name, because it would be absorbed into the surrounding farmland and merge inconspicuously into the existing agricultural landscape. Its owners had decided to enclose it.

The intention was to split the Heath up into lots, some of which would be distributed proportionately amongst those who claimed grazing rights on the land while the remainder would be sold off. Discussions among interested parties took place over a number of years and in 1800 a proposal for partition was put before Cardiff Corporation. After some discussion it was accepted on the strong recommendation of John Wood, a solicitor of Duke Street, who was also town clerk of Cardiff and would shortly purchase much of the Heath for himself.

What was the motive behind the decision to inclose and partially sell off the Great Heath? William Rees was of the opinion that it was a shortsighted response to a change of circumstances. Cardiff Corporation were in need of money; they were anxious to pay off a loan of £450 from the Marquess of Bute which, with interest, had risen to £700 by 1800, and they were also seeking funds to complete the new Market Hall near St John's church. Cardiff's residents had become less dependent upon farming over the centuries and demand for pasture rights on the Heath had dwindled, so much so, that the corporation had adopted the practice of leasing grazing rights to individuals at annual auctions. Selling the common rights on the Heath would raise the money the corporation needed and rid the burgesses of what they had come to view as an increasingly useless asset.

The momentous decision to enclose the Great Heath did not pass by peacefully. Over the centuries the area of open common had gradually dwindled as people fenced off small plots for themselves. These were usually poor people seeking a foothold where they could set up a home for themselves and their families and who had possibly been influenced by the belief, widely held in parts of Wales, that if someone began constructing a house on common ground after sunset, succeeded in roofing it and have smoke rising from the chimney by sunrise, he would own it. This was the 'Tŷ Unnos' ('Over-night House'). A surrounding plot of ground within an axe-throw from the door could also be enclosed and kept. Thousands of needy families had been helped by gangs of friends or relatives to create homes for themselves in this way.

Reaction to encroachment on commons was ambivalent. In some areas landowners closed their eyes to the practice for a variety of reasons, in others they allowed cottages built in this way to remain on payment of an annual rent. Eighteenth-century corporation rent rolls show that Cardiff imposed rental fines on private squatters on the Heath and, subsequently, claimed ownership of their houses 'in the public interest'. Some owners resorted to eviction whenever instances of encroachment came to their attention, a practice approved of by Walter Davies in his report on South Wales to the Board of Agriculture of 1815:

> Open wastes are considered as obstacles as they encourage a kind of independence which is too commonly the parent of idleness in the lower class who dwell on their borders or have erected cottages and made encroachments upon them.[1]

Before the decision to enclose the Great Heath was taken, the Marquess of Bute, as lord of the manor of Llystalybont, had already taken steps to establish the legal position locally. He had taken up a test prosecution in 1797 against a squatter who had encroached on the Heath and had won his case. Encouraged by this favourable verdict he took proceedings against a further twelve encroachers the following year. Feelings ran high when the court ruled that Daniel Jones, acting on behalf of the twelve, was too late in filing his defence and the verdict went in favour of the prosecution once again. Observers believed that the squatters had lost their case on a technicality.

It is no surprise that the situation was tense on the morning of 12 June 1799, when the under-sheriff decided to enforce the declarations of eviction against the twelve. The following account of events was written in his diary by John Bird, steward to the Marquess of Bute, who was present on that day and also made a second visit on 30 July, to provide the Marquess with a record of the outcome of the day's activities:

> This morning was fixed upon by Mr Wood and Mr Williams, for the Deputy Sheriff, for taking down the twelve cottages and enclosures on the Great and Little Heath, which had suffered judgement.
>
> Considerable resistance was made for more than two hours and the consequences were very disagreeable till I was dispatched to Town by the Under Sheriff for the assistance of the cavalry: upon whose appearance, headed by Mr Wyndham Lewis, Mr Powell Edwards and Capt. Wood, after taking one of the ringleaders into custody the hostile part of the mob began to disperse—but as the Under Sheriff was apprehensive that a greater body would assemble in the evening I was dispatched express to Caerphilly and Energlyn for the assistance of their Volunteers. Mr Goodrich, as Sheriff, immediately returned with me and directed his son

---

[1] W. Davies, *General View of the Agriculture and Domestic Economy of South Wales* (1815), ii. 482.

and the other officers to be as expeditious as possible in bringing down the Volunteers who immediately mustered. When we got to the hill [i.e. Thornhill] above Newhouse I discovered that the cottage where the greatest resistance had been made had been put on fire as the most effective method of destroying it and when we came to the third milestone from Cardiff we found that the appearance of the cavalry had entirely dispersed the most hostile part of the mob and that the Under Sheriff and his Bailiffs with Mr Bew and your [i.e. Lord Bute's] workmen had been joined by a competent number of stout fellows from Cardiff who were desirous of giving all the assistance in their power and that the Caerphilly Volunteers were not now wanted as the cottagers were all appealing for pardon and time to remove their goods etc ... One month has been granted them for that purpose when the twelve who are to be evicted are to abandon them. Dr Griffiths's house will come down, being one of the number, and possession has been given to you by the Sheriff of the remaining eleven which are only standing on sufferance for one month. The women, for some time, acted the part of Amazonians, having armed themselves with pitchforks, etc ... etc ...

Bird recorded his second visit thus:

30th July, 1799. The High Sheriff, Mr Goodrich, and his deputy, Mr Williams, with Mr Vaughan, Attorney, and Mr Bew, the workmen, horses, chains and implements for pulling down, etc ... went to the Heath for the purpose of destroying the cottages of those who had not signed the petition for leave to remain till the 19th of October next. I attended to identify the premises and the four who had not signed were very glad to come into the same terms as the others. The best part of a hedge and bank was destroyed and burnt in the presence of the Sheriff which had been erected by a man not included in the twelve but who had on several occasions behaved with insolence.

The third milestone from Cardiff mentioned by Bird was a significant marker on the turnpike road to Caerphilly. By the end of the eighteenth century the road had been divided into three-mile sections, each of which was maintained by a member of the trust. In February 1783 the trust ordered that 'the sum of £20 be paid to the Revd William Lewellin for repairing the North Road leading from Cardiff to the third milestone on the Heath ... Also ordered that £20 be paid to William Lewis, Esq. for repairing the road from Cardiff Common [i.e. the Heath] to Caerffilley Common'. The milestone, faintly inscribed 'From Cardiff III mile', could be seen prior to November 1999, set into the stone wall which used to flank Caerphilly Road about fifteen yards north of its junction with Maes-y-coed Road. This wall formed part of the outbuildings of the old Mynydd Bychan (later called Ton-yr-ywen) farm, demolished in the

9 The eighteenth-century milestone on Caerphilly Road near the junction with Maes-y-coed Road.

mid 1940s to make way for the Gnome photographic products factory. When this section of road was widened in December 1999, the milestone, along with a nineteenth-century cast-iron counterpart, was reset into the brick boundary wall of the new Lidl supermarket, slightly to the east of the demolished stone wall.

John Bird's account explains how local opposition to enclosure had been swiftly overcome. The way was now open for the corporation to carry out its intentions by putting forward a Bill outlining its proposals in Parliament. It was accepted and in 1801 'An Act for Dividing, Allotting and Inclosing the several Common, Waste and Heath Lands commonly known by the names of the Great and Little Heaths, otherwise Mwynydd Bychan and Wain Dyfal, lying within the parishes of Saint John the Baptist in Cardiff, Llandaff, Whitchurch, Roath and Llanishen in the County of Glamorgan' was passed. This gave the corporation authority to proceed.

The corporation began by drawing up an award which allotted land to each of the freeholders entitled to rights of pasture on the Heath, leaving a residue of land which would be sold off.[1] Cardiff Corporation received the major allotment of 330 acres, representing half the available land. The first Marquess of Bute and his heir obtained 33 acres as lords of the manors of Cardiff and Llystalybont, and a further allotment of 48 acres as freeholders with rights of pasture. Other landowners also received substantial allotments for their rights: 63 acres to the Lewis family of Llanishen, 37 acres to Charles Morgan of Ruperra, 20 acres to William Williams, and 10 acres to John Kemeys Tynte. Other plots of land, ranging from 8 acres to fractions of an acre, were granted to a further 26 claimants. The remainder of the Great Heath was sold by auction on 6 and 7 November 1801 at the Cardiff Arms Hotel. A map of 1803 (Plate 11) shows that substantial parcels of land were bought by John Goodrich, Henry Hollier, John Wood, James Harford, John Harford and William Richards, who were either local landowners or rich and influential men. More modest plots were sold to John Bird, Henry Barry, Charles Vachell, William Rowland, Barbara Williams, William Roberts, Richard Price Williams, William Jones, Edward Williams and Llewelin Prosser.

The corporation ensured that its share contained the racecourse in order to

---

[1] The map and award are available for inspection at the Glamorgan Record Office.

safeguard the future of racing there. As soon as all the allocations had been made the burgesses voted to transfer a proportion of their lands to the Marquess of Bute in an attempt to reduce their debt to him—an inadequate gesture, it appears, for the debt had risen to £1,000 by 1819. They were more successful when they devoted money to their building fund since the new market was completed in 1835.

The Heath landscape was transformed during the first decade or so of the nineteenth century. It was split up into fields and plots of land demarcated by low earthen banks topped with rapid-growing hedges of quickthorn with occasional groves of trees. Access to the racecourse was preserved by classifying the old tracks which formerly crossed the Heath as public rights of way; one track running through the middle of the racecourse followed the line of the old road across the Heath while another skirted south of the racecourse. They were both unnamed at that time but today the former has become Heathwood Road and the latter Heath Park Lane at its Caerphilly Road end, continuing as the lane behind St Angela Road before disappearing under the University Hospital at its Allensbank Road end. Whitchurch Road and Allensbank Roads were also unnamed tracks running along the perimeter of the Heath at this time; they, too, were carefully numbered on the 1803 map and clearly denoted as public rights of way. In 1805 Whitchurch Road was described as 'the new road from Roath Church to the 2-mile milestone [i.e. on Caerphilly Road]

10 Ton-yr-ywen Farm, as sketched for *Cardiff Records.*

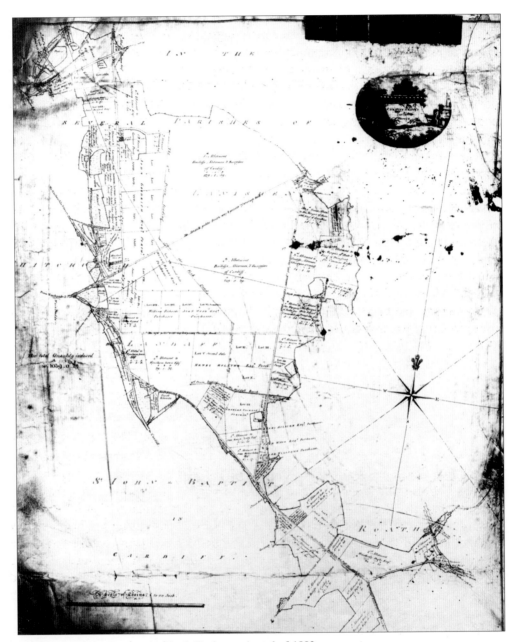

11 The map accompanying the Heath Enclosure Award of 1803.

on the Heath'.[1]

Caerphilly Road, of course, was an ancient highway and was then being maintained by a turnpike trust but it appears that the local parish vestries were rather reluctant to accept the responsibility of maintaining the new roads set out during enclosure. A survey carried out in the parish of Llandaff in 1837 declared that the roads represented nowadays by Heath Park Lane, Allensbank Road and Whitchurch Road were nothing better than rough tracks which would need an expenditure of £66 in order to bring them up to scratch.[2]

The roads in Llanishen parish were probably in better condition because those now represented by Heath Halt Road and Heath Park Avenue had been made up by the second Marquess of Bute at the request of the parish vestry, which in September 1823 resolved to give Lord Bute £15 a year for three years, 'providing that he makes a road equal to any in this parish, except the Highway, from Rhyd Lydan [the ford beneath the present Three Arches bridge] to the land on the south side of the Race Course on the Heath', i.e. down to the parish boundary.[3]

At the opening of the nineteenth century the Great Heath saw a brief but radical period of transformation which was followed by almost a century of stability. The early years of the twentieth century saw the onset of another, but different, type of transformation which has maintained its impetus throughout the century.

The Lewis Family

As a result of enclosure, several local families acquired land which had previously formed part of the Heath. The one which was to be most closely associated with the subsequent development of the area was the Lewis family, descendants of the medieval Welsh rulers of Senghennydd, whose seat was the mansion at Y Fan (The Van) near Caerphilly. A younger son of the Lewis family married an heiress from Llanishen in the early seventeenth century and built a house there, originally simply called Llanishen House. It later became Old House, after Thomas Lewis, one of the descendants, married the heiress of Rhiwbina and Cefn Carnau lands situated on the high ground north of Cardiff, rebuilt Dan-y-ddraenen farm on Thornhill and renamed it New House. This Thomas Lewis had gained fame and fortune in the late eighteenth century as one of the founders of Dowlais Ironworks at Merthyr Tydfil.

During the eighteenth and early nineteenth centuries the Lewis family of both Old House and New House bought land in Llanishen and neighbouring parishes, much of it part of the former Great Heath and its environs, which had come on the market

---

[1] Edgar L. Chappell, 'Notes on Cardiff Turnpike Trust' (MS. in Cardiff Central Library).

[2] An Account of the Roads in the Parish of Llandaff (1837).

[3] Llanishen Parish Vestry Book, 22 Sept. 1823.

because the enclosure of the Heath had prompted a series of sales. The Lewises of Llanishen succeeded in building an extensive estate and became a family of standing and influence locally.

The succession at Old House came to an end when Wyndham Lewis died a bachelor in 1835. Shortly afterwards, the estate was sold to the Marquess of Bute who demolished the house to make way for Llanishen Fawr Farm. It appears that much, if not all, of the proceeds of the sale, along with a great deal of land; passed into the possession of the other branch of the Lewis family who were still living at New House.

Most of that fortune ultimately seems to have been inherited by the Revd W. Price Lewis (1779–1848), youngest son of the family born at New House during the closing years of the eighteenth century. His older brothers and sisters had already inherited their father's home and property at New House, their mother's home and property at Parc, Capel Llanillterne, and other property through marriage at Tongwynlais and elsewhere. By 1843 almost all the land of the former Great Heath was owned by the Revd W.P. Lewis as his part of the family inheritance. The tithe maps of the 1840s for Whitchurch, Llanishen, Llandaff and Cardiff (St John's) show that all the ground lying between Allensbank Road in the east and Caerphilly Road in the west, and between Tŷ Glas Road in the north and Whitchurch Road in the south, was owned or leased by him. This estate probably represented a combination of Old House and New House lands.

By this time, the Great Heath had undergone the greatest transformation of its long history. A patchwork of fields devoted to cultivation and pasture interspersed with groves of trees had replaced the original open ground. Three farms, Allen's Bank (at the junction of the present-day Allensbank Road and Inglefield Avenue), Heath (the site of Heath Woodland) and Mynydd Bychan (later called Ton-yr-ywen, at the junction of Maes-y-coed Road and Caerphilly Road), and two cottages, Heath Cottage (beneath St Edwen Gardens) and Ton-yr-ywen Cottages (beneath the former British Oxygen plant) are to be seen on the 1 in. Ordnance Survey map of 1833. These were all built after enclosure, except Mynydd Bychan Farm, which appears on a late eighteenth-century map and must have been an old encroachment.

The Revd W.P. Lewis built a large new house for himself, sometime between 1835 and 1840, at or near the Heath Farm and named it Heathfield. Later it came to be known as Heath House. Heath Farm was later relocated within the northern half of the racecourse alongside the lane (now Heathwood Road) which ran east–west across it. The lane running south of the racecourse from the Cross Inn, Gabalfa, to Allensbank Road was adapted to form a wide tree-lined carriageway. It led from an elaborate entrance off North Road, then ran along the line of the modern Heath Park Lane before sweeping northwards to Heath House itself. A lodge at the North Road entrance was occupied by Thomas Redcliffe in the 1920s and 1930s.

When W.P. Lewis died in 1848, he bequeathed Heath House and its land to his 21-year-old nephew, Wyndham William Lewis (1827–71) of Parc House, Capel Llanillterne. He was to live there for 23 years until his death at the early age of 44.

One of his first actions after gaining partial control of the estate in 1849 was to pay Cardiff Corporation £3,100 for 157 acres of land north of the modern Heathwood Road which contained the upper half of the racecourse. Heath Farm may, consequently, have been moved from its original site near to (or beneath) Heath House in order to manage this extensive additional portion of farmland. He was to maintain the Lewis family's practice of increasing its estates in the area north of Cardiff.

Wyndham William Lewis was educated at Worcester College, Oxford, and trained for the legal profession. He was soon to be deeply involved in the administrative and social life of Glamorgan. In 1850 he married his first wife, Annie Overton of Llanddety Hall near Brecon, and their daughter, Annie Mary Price Lewis, was born the following year. His first wife suffered constant ill-health and the family would habitually spend the winter months at a rented mansion close to the milder sea air of Weston-super-Mare.

W.W. Lewis possessed a charismatic personality. He was generous and sociable and in 1855, aged only 28, his widespread popularity gained for him the cherished office of high sheriff of Glamorgan. A report of the high sheriff's dinner (*Cardiff and Merthyr Guardian*, 7 July 1855) indicates the respect which his fellow gentry felt for their young sheriff:

This event took place at the Angel Hotel at 3.00 p.m. and was in every respect a sumptuous feast ... The High Sheriff's Band was in attendance in the lobby and also performed during the dinner and between the toasts. Upwards of 150 gentlemen sat down, the High Sheriff presiding ...

The time left for speaking was limited, and toasts given on the occasion were necessarily proposed and responded to in a very brief manner. Nash Vaughan Edwards Vaughan, Esq. proposed 'THE HIGH SHERIFF' which was the signal for a most enthusiastic outburst of feeling. The High Sheriff's health having been drunk upstanding with nine times nine and one cheer more that gentleman rose to acknowledge the compliment AND WAS AGAIN RECEIVED WITH DEAFENING APPLAUSE ... The High Sheriff resumed his seat amid vehement applause ...

The High Sheriff arose and said that he must depart for the South Wales Railway Station to meet the Lord Chief Justice. He was obliged to leave the company but his excellent friend, Mr. Jenner, had kindly consented to occupy his place as chairman at his request. Although the company entertained the highest respect for Mr. Jenner ... their high regard for Wyndham Lewis would not allow them to adopt the suggestion and allow the High Sheriff to depart alone. The company AROSE EN MASSE TO ACCOMPANY HIM TO THE STATION and in a very few minutes the spacious room was empty and a procession formed in Angel Street which escorted him to the platform of the railway ...

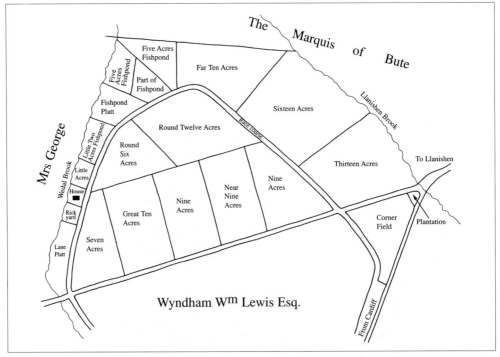

12 G.S. Strawson's plan of 1849 showing land purchased by W.W. Lewis from Cardiff Corporation, including the northern half of the racecourse to the north of the modern Heathwood Road.

Contemporary magazines and newspapers contain references to his habitual appearances at race meetings, banquets and other social events. In 1850 he was appointed joint-trustee of the Llanishen parish charity fund, which sought to help local paupers. He was responsible for inaugurating the Llanishen Ploughing Society in an effort to promote improved farming practice within the parish. His favourite pastime, however, was fox-hunting. He brought the Parc Hunt dogs with him when he moved to the Heath in 1848 and soon gained widespread renown as the Master of the Heath Hounds. The 1875 Ordnance Survey map shows that his kennels were located downwind from the house at a site now occupied by Crystal Avenue. He planted trees on selected tracts of his estate in order to preserve all kinds of game. The most extensive of these was the 40-acre Crystal Covert which also contained a round summer house with wide paths radiating from it. This was probably planted in the early 1850s in the Far Ten Acre Field, Sixteen Acre Field, and Thirteen Acre Field indicated on Strawson's map of 1849. Does its rather unusual name have any connection with the opening of Crystal Palace in 1851 to house the Great Exhibition? Several modern streets on the Heath bear the name of this covert.

An extract from *The Field* (20 January 1872) shows how popular the Heath had become for local hunts:

13 An early photograph of Heath House from the west.

> The hounds met at the Heath, the residence of the late Mr Wyndham Lewis. The fox was found in the Crystal Plantation and after running around Heath House it broke away to the north to the adjoining plantations and into a small brake at the side of the road to Thornhill where it waited for us. Then we ran him hard into the gorse beyond New House. He then made as if to go to Tongwynlais, sinking the valley straight over the mountain for the forest but when three hundred yards from it he turned short to the left crossing the bottom to Caerphilly Station. He then bore left to Taff's Well over the summit of Castell Coch into a large covert where another fox jumped up. The pack divided with the main body driving the first fox into an old quarry below the castle where it went to ground. The hounds did not reach home until well after dark.

After each sporting event held at the Heath, Wyndham Lewis would entertain lavishly at the House. His own 'SAX-TUBA BAND', led by G.F. Davies of Duke Street, Cardiff, provided light music at these events, one of the favourite pieces played by them being the 'Heath Waltz' specially composed for Wyndham Lewis by their leader. They had taken part in the High Sheriff's Dinner at the Angel Hotel and had led a civic procession up the drive from North Road to Heath House in 1859, as the

Cardiff Times (13 August 1859) reported:

> Wednesday was a festive day at Heath Mansion, the residence of
> Wyndham W. Lewis Esq. who has now come into possession of those
> estates which give him a high social position within the county ... An
> address was prepared ... Preparations were also made for a large pro-
> cession of carriages from Cardiff to the Heath to present the address...
>
> The corporation took the lead in three carriages and then came a
> miscellaneous host ... numbering upwards of fifty. The procession passed
> up High Street, Duke Street and Crockherbtown to Plucca Lane by which
> circuitous route they gained North Road and so on to the Heath.
>
> Messrs Bachelor's band played at the head of the procession as far as
> the end of Crockherbtown whence it proceeded to the North Road to await
> it. On arriving at the drive leading to the Heath[1] Mr Lewis's band met the
> procession which passed through a triumphal arch to the private carriage-
> way. Here the sun shone beauteously and as the carriages passed slowly
> along the circuitous path, their occupants got a good view of the
> cavalcade. A large number of per-
> sons had arrived at the mansion
> before the procession and when all
> had alighted and a semicircle had
> been formed in front of the hall Mr
> and Mrs Lewis and their daughter
> came forward to receive the address
> from the mayor. The family were
> loudly cheered.

The grounds surrounding the house
were landscaped. Trees, including the tall
pines which were becoming fashionable at
that time, were planted in groves. Gravel
paths wound between lawns, shrubberies
and flower-beds and a fishpond was sited
quite near the house. Behind the house
was a substantial stable block. The site of
the house today lies beneath the car park
between the minature railway and the mini
golf course in Heath Park. The fish pond
is still in existence.

14 The Lewis family grave in Llanishen churchyard.

Wyndham Lewis's first wife, having

---

[1] i.e. near the present Cross Inn.

endured ill-health for many years, died in 1864. He married his second wife, Maud Williams of Aberpergwm House in the Vale of Neath, in 1867. She, too, was an accomplished horsewoman. Their wedding in London was a fashionable event, as the *Cambrian* (8 March 1867) reported:

> Great interest was excited in Cardiff and the surrounding district on Monday last by news of the marriage having taken place in the morning of that day at St George's, Hanover Square, of Wyndham W. Lewis, Esq., of the Heath, Llanishen, to Maud, youngest daughter of the late W. Williams, Esq., of Aberpergwm. Mr Lewis is not only the head of one of the most ancient and distinguished families of the county, but one of the most extensive landowners of the district, and withal an affable and kindly gentleman who mingles freely with other people without the air of conferring a favour by gracious condescension. He is consequently popular not only with his own tenantry but with townsfolk and country people in general; and it is years since such a display of bunting has been seen in Cardiff as was made on Monday last in compliment to him. Flags streamed in every street and in many an evening company health and happiness to the wedded pair were drunk. St John's bells rang merrily all day. At the Heath there was a dinner and festivities of the tenantry and neighbours …

Wyndham Lewis continued to add to his estate. In 1869 he bought New House and 450 acres of land in the parishes of Llanishen and Whitchurch from his widowed aunt for £12,000. Tragically, he died a week or so before the birth of his second daughter, Charlotte Eleanor, in September 1871 and was buried in Llanishen churchyard, as the *Cardiff and Merthyr Guardian* (16 September 1871) reported:

> We regret to announce the death of Mr Wyndham Lewis at his residence The Heath. For some few years past the deceased gentleman had been in failing health … his hospitality when in health was almost unbounded. Few men have probably enjoyed more local popularity than Mr Wyndham Lewis and the ovation that he received on the occasion of his filling of the office of the High Sheriff of the County will not easily be forgotten by those who witnessed it. The remains of the deceased gentleman were interred on Thursday in a new vault in the pretty churchyard of Llanishen …

Plate 14 shows the Lewis family memorial near the north gate of the churchyard, emblazoned with the family arms and motto, 'Ofner na ofno angau' ('Fear him who fears not death'). The east window above the altar was erected in Wyndham Lewis's memory in 1873. He was a man who made his name a household word in the Cardiff area and made The Heath a byword in the social circles of Glamorgan.

The Bute Brickworks

As landownership on the Great Heath went through a period of change during the early nineteenth century the second Marquess of Bute was consolidating his estate on its fringes. In 1818 he acquired the 280-acre estate of his former agent, Henry Hollier, including the lands of Penylan and Rhyd-y-pennau farms, and in 1826 purchased the Llanishen House estate which included the lands of Tŷ Glas Farm (off Tŷ Glas Road).

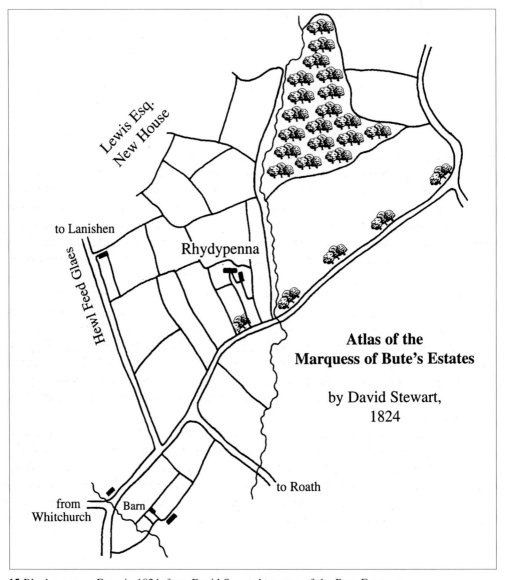

15 Rhyd-y-pennau Farm in 1824, from David Stewart's survey of the Bute Estate.

Together, this amounted to a huge swathe of territory lying immediately north and east of the former Great Heath. David Stewart's survey of the Bute Estate in 1824 (Plate 15) marks an unnamed building at the point where the road over the Great Heath from Rhyd-y-pennau to the Birchgrove Inn forded Llanishen Brook. On a map of the Llanishen House Estate by William Morrice of 1777 this can be identified as a pair of stone cottages named Rhyd Lydan. They were on land belonging to Tŷ Glas Farm which, as part of the Llanishen House Estate, was purchased by Lord Bute in 1826.

In 1851 these cottages were occupied by David Roberts and Richard Turner, two young men who had brought their wives from the Newtown area of Montgomeryshire to live in Cardiff. David Roberts was described in the census as a pipe-maker. Did he carry on his trade at his Rhyd Lydan home? There would be hardly enough room for a workshop in addition to family accommodation in a typical nineteenth-century cottage. It seems most likely that he had already become involved in some form of local clay-working venture.

Ten years later it appears that David Roberts or an associate had expanded the little works at Rhyd Lydan, since he is described as a brick and tile maker in the census. As a local writer observed in 1896, 'The clays of the district are well suited for brick-making ... Those of the Old Red Sandstone are occasionally used, as at Maindy and Llanishen, and are said to make a fair brick of light red colour'.[1]

It was not Lord Bute's practice to set up his own industries on his own land. His experience as a result of sinking coal mines on his Durham estate had made him very wary of that type of venture; thereafter, he preferred to lease his lands for others to set up industries or build houses. He believed that it was safer and easier to claim rent from his lessees and royalties from businesses. On this basis, the company near Rhyd Lydan would either have paid a levy per ton of clay dug or on the finished product (for example, 1s. per 1,000 bricks or tiles) to the Bute Estate.

Plate 16 shows the site of the brickworks from Heath Halt in 1929. Heath Halt Road runs down the foreground and Heathwood Road across the middle of the photograph. The site of the brickworks lies in the big field on the right and is occupied today by the Three Arches Garage and the houses between it and Rhyd-y-pennau Crossroads. The depression near the white bungalows in the field in the centre of the photograph is the edge of an early claypit dug by the brickworks company; Three Arches Avenue traverses it today. A later claypit lies just off the right-hand margin of the photograph.

The company needed a reliable supply of water in order to maintain their output. Its primary use was for mixing with the newly dug clay to ensure a suitable consistency prior to the moulding process but it was also vital for use in the boilers which provided energy for the whole process. All machinery at that time was steam-driven. The company therefore made a reservoir by damming a little stream with a clay bank and channelling the water down to their works. When the Caerphilly to

---

[1] *Cardiff: an Illustrated Handbook* (ed. J. Ballinger) (1896).

16 The site of the abandoned Bute Brickworks, seen from the Rhymney Railway embankment, with Heath Halt Road in the foreground.

Cardiff section of the Rhymney Railway was opened in 1871 its embankment cut across this channel and the contractors had to ensure that water supply was maintained by piping it through the new obstruction. Today, the reservoir bed has been drained and it forms part of the site of St Brigid's Roman Catholic church in the Crystals which was opened in 1964 to replace a temporary building a few hundred yards to the south.

What was of more concern, however was that the path of the new railway embankment would take it directly over the two Rhyd Lydan stone cottages. They stood where the northern abutment of the Three Arches Bridge lies today. In 1870 or thereabouts they were demolished and rebuilt in brick at a T-junction on the Rhyd-y-pennau Road (which has since developed into a crossroads) and were variously known as Rhyd Lydan Cottages, Brickyard Cottages or Bute Cottages. Today they are occupied by a hairdresser's salon. Dare we presume that they were built of bricks made in the brickyard on the opposite side of the road? David Roberts, Richard Turner and their families moved with their homes, for in 1881 and 1891 they were living at Brickyard Cottages and both men were described as brickmakers.

During this first phase of existence the Bute Brickworks was limited to producing standard common bricks. One of these early bricks can be seen today alongside the pavement in Heol Hir, Llanishen. This rare example, set into the corner pillar of the wall fronting Elm Cottage (No 18), has been thoughtfully preserved in order to display its bold BUTE stamp. In about 1889 the brickworks was taken over by another company with its head office at 16 St John's Chambers in St John's Square in the town centre and renamed the Duffryn & Llanishen Brick, Tile, Sanitary Pipe & Terra Cotta Company, which also owned another brickyard at Aberdare and was managed by Tyeth D. Bounsall. The title adopted by the new company indicates that production at the brickworks was set to expand and diversify. An article in the *Cardiff Argus* (5 July 1890), explains how the 10-acre site had been dramatically improved since being taken over:

> The Llanishen works were formerly used simply for the manufacture of common bricks, but since being acquired by this company, the property, covering upwards of ten acres, has been considerably developed, more than £3,000 having been spent in this direction, in fact the place has been entirely transformed and presents an altogether different aspect from what it did a year or so ago.
>
> The clay used here (about 100 tons a day) is obtained from a large pit (drained by a powerful steam pump) already 36 feet deep and proved to 30 feet lower. From this pit it is hauled up a gantry about 200 feet long to a large clay mill fitted with patent hauling gear worked by friction pulleys. The tram is made to tip its load into the mill by a neat automatic contrivance, which means a great saving of labour. After going through this mill the clay is mixed with water by special machinery and then passed through one of Whitehead's horizontal brick machines which is capable of turning out 25,000 bricks per day. The bricks, cut off by wire, ten at a time, are then placed on barrows and stacked in large drying warehouses having iron plated floors which are heated by means of the exhaust steam from the engine. One of these buildings holds no less than 30,000 bricks and a considerable quantity, something like 150,000 are stacked on waste ground, being matted over and covered with light timber during stormy weather. For the purposes of burning there are three patent down-draught kilns, holding about 50,000 each, built on the most modern principles and it was noticed that the bricks, as they were being taken out of one of these were practically perfect throughout the kiln. The output is about 100,000 per week and it may be mentioned that it is of these bricks that the Rhondda Sewer is made as also several other drainage and engineering projects throughout the country…
>
> But that which proved the most interesting feature in these works was undoubtedly the terra-cotta department. Here was stacked a quantity of specially prepared clay which was being pressed into various shaped moulds by a number of workmen. After a mould is well-filled it is allowed to stand for some hours, the contents then being carefully tipped out on to a stand and finished up by hand until ready for 'burning' … The terra-cotta goods, which for the most part are of artistic designs drawn by architects, are placed in a special patent muffled kiln something like an

17 A brick made at the Bute Brickworks.

oven ...

The kiln is entered by a door which is bricked up when in work and the peculiarity is that no fire can possibly touch the clay, being separated from it by a wall through which the heat penetrates. We were just in time to see the contents of this kiln being discharged, consisting of such things as chimney pots, ridge tiles, finials, coping blocks &c. of various kinds and patterns. The workmanship all appeared good and the colour very rich. This, we understand, is entirely new work introduced by the Company and is likely to prove a very important feature of the undertaking. All the goods from these works which have to go by rail are carted to either Llanishen or Llandaff Stations, according to their destination.

The new company's hopes of an improvement in business were not realised for it had ceased production within a decade. Although an entry for R. Turner, brickmaker, Bute Cottages, can be found in the *Cardiff Directory* for 1899, no trace of the works appears on the Ordnance Survey map of 1900. When contractors' carts engaged in the construction of the Cardiff Railway were cutting up a footpath beside the brickworks reservoir Llanishen parish council demanded its repair and referred to the reservoir as the 'Old Brickyard Pond'. It was called the 'disused brickyard pond' in February 1906, when councillors asked the Bute Estate to prevent water, which was eroding the footpath, from escaping from it.[1] What could have caused the company's demise

---

[1] Glamorgan Record Office, Llanishen parish council minutes, 30 Jan. 1900, 1 Feb. 1906.

during Cardiff's house-building boom? Did it encounter unforeseen problems at the Dyffryn site? Did the demand for terracotta fail to materialise or was business overwhelmed by competition from other yards such as the Phoenix Brickworks on Caerphilly Road?

The inscriptions on two gravestones near the western door of Llanishen church give poignant testimony to a lifetime's association with the brickworks:

Sacred to the Memory of
Elizabeth, wife of David Roberts
Bute Brickworks, Llanishen
Who died March 3rd, 1891
Aged 76 years
Also, the above David Roberts
Who died January 18th, 1898
Aged 78 years

Sacred to the memory of
Richard Turner
Who died Sept. 24th, 1899
Aged 78 years
Also, Mary, his Wife
Who died December 28th, 1908
Aged 82 years

Two Railways

The railways of South Wales developed in part as the result of fierce competition between companies intent on capturing the highly profitable traffic of the coalfield. The Taff Vale Railway was the first to appear, built in 1841 by the Merthyr ironmasters to replace the Glamorganshire Canal which they had originally built to carry iron from their works down the Taff valley for shipment at its estuary below Cardiff. All the land along the shoreline belonged to the second Marquess of Bute who had heard of the plans to build the new railway and had opened his West Dock in 1839 in anticipation of the increased traffic it would bring. He granted the railway company sole use of the eastern half of his dock on condition that they would never transfer their trade to any other dock company. Lord Bute had timed it perfectly: from 1840 onwards the iron trade was being rivalled by the rapid growth of the coal trade which by the end of the century had made Cardiff the greatest coal-exporting port in the world. The development of the Heath, however, was more directly affected by two other railways.

Rhymney Railway

The Rhymney Railway roughly demarcates the present eastern boundary of the Heath district. After the death of the second Marquess of Bute in 1848 trustees acting on behalf of his infant son followed his policy of seeking to maintain a Bute monopoly of the export trade from the Taff, Rhondda and Cynon valleys of the coalfield. The Taff Vale Railway was already carrying all the coal from the existing mines in these valleys to the West Dock; it was now time to look for additional trade from newly developing sources in the Eastern Valleys.

Their prime target was the Rhymney Valley. The Bute Estate had a large stake in the Rhymney Ironworks, which used a horse tramway to carry its output to Newport for shipment. Furthermore, the estate owned large tracts of land in the valley which the trustees wished to lease to coal prospectors. A railway was the vital element needed to capitalise on the valley's rich resources. Consequently, the Bute Trustees urged the Rhymney Ironworks to build a railway down the valley to Cardiff. As an inducement they opened a larger and more modern East Dock in 1855–9, the use of which they offered to the proposed new railway company at very reasonable rates.

The iron company responded by forming the Rhymney Railway Company. Work started after the necessary capital had been raised and the track was laid southward to Caerphilly. There, however, the company was forced to compromise since the great mass of Caerphilly Mountain barred their way directly south. It would have been too expensive to tunnel through the mountain and so they diverted their track westward, through the Nantgarw gap into the Taff valley where they had been given Parliamentary powers to connect with the TVR at Taff's Well and run their trains down to Cardiff on the existing track. At Cardiff, they diverted their trains back on to their own track which carried them across to the new East Dock via a short extension line. The first train from Rhymney to Cardiff ran on 25 February 1858.

This arrangement soon began to sour relationships between all parties concerned. The TVR envied the more efficient facilities offered cheaply to the Rhymney Railway at the East Dock. They had outgrown the West Dock where restricted capacity and old-fashioned loading appliances were causing expensive delay and frustration. When they sought permission from the Bute Trustees to divert their excess traffic to East Dock they were refused. The trustees had secret intentions to attract even more mineral trade from other Monmouthshire valleys and were hoping to accommodate it at the East Dock.

The TVR retaliated by instigating a vendetta against the Rhymney. They began by charging an unauthorised levy on all Rhymney trains arriving at Cardiff and delaying trains waiting to join their track at Taff's Well. These difficulties aggravated a serious financial problem which had overtaken the Rhymney company. They had overspent on the construction of their railway but, to make matters worse, the coal trade from the Rhymney valley had still not developed sufficiently to generate returns which could compensate adequately for their crippling outlay. Rhymney shareholders began to protest at the continued lack of paid dividends.

The outlook was so bleak that the company considered plans to sell up but before acting upon them they decided to make a bold but risky attempt to save the railway. They revived their original intention of running their track directly south from Caerphilly to Cardiff by means of a tunnel under the mountain and a final appeal for money was made to their shareholders. The latter remained loyal, the necessary funds and parliamentary approval were received, and work on the final leg of the railway began. It was completed in 1871 and the first train to use the new route ran on 1 April of that year.

The gamble was a total success. It enabled the company to eliminate their costly and contentious detour into the Taff Valley. By now the new mines of the Rhymney valley were ready to begin production. The opening of the new route to Cardiff had been perfectly timed and the fortunes of the Rhymney shareholders took a turn for the better. They received consistently good dividends until the railway went out of existence following the First World War when the coalfield companies were amalgamated with the Great Western Railway by Act of Parliament of 1921.

After leaving Caerphilly Tunnel the Rhymney Railway traversed a wide belt of gentle countryside before reaching Cardiff. It descended on a 1 in 80 gradient, part of which lay on an embankment which, in places, was as much as 60 feet high. Operating rules were strict for coal trains beginning their descent to Cardiff. They had to stop before entering Llanishen station, the only one between Caerphilly and Cardiff, where a strategically based banksman would help the guard pin down the brakes on all the wagons in order to prevent the train careering out of control down the gradient. It would often need two locomotives pulling in front and a third pushing at the rear to bring the empty wagons back up the track from Cardiff to the tunnel.

Despite the company's admirable code of practice, accidents did occur. On 10 May 1912 a coal train bound for the docks left the tunnel above the permitted speed because its total weight of 650 tons had already begun to overpower the locomotive's holding power. It failed to stop at Llanishen station, preventing the banksman from pinning down the brakes on the wagons, and began careering down the line at 40 miles an hour. The driver put the engine into reverse but despite this the train continued to gain momentum. At Heath Junction a train from Coryton carrying 33 pasengers was preparing to join the Rhymney line but the driver, hearing the frantic warning whistles of the approaching runaway, stopped his train in the nick of time. His prompt action averted what could have been a major disaster and he was duly rewarded by the GWR for his alertness. Meanwhile, the coal train had reached a speed of 60 miles per hour but warnings had been sent ahead and tracks cleared. It roared through the former Parade Station near Newport Road and almost reached the docks when it crashed into the rear of another coal train stopped at a signal. The impact caused severe damage to the track and a large number of coal wagons, while 'the runaway engine, buckled into an almost shapeless mass, formed the central figure of

18 A coal train crossing Llanishen Viaduct in 1904.

the huge pile of debris'.[1] Luckily, the driver and fireman managed to jump clear at the last moment and succeeded in escaping with minor injuries.

Below Llanishen the Rhymney Railway crossed a single-arched bridge over Fidlas Road (the second arch was opened in 1932) before traversing a high three-arched bridge, known originally as Llanishen Viaduct; this crossed the spot where the narrow cart-track over the Heath to the Birchgrove Inn forded Llanishen brook at Rhyd Lydan. On its way southward the railway ran on Bute lands east of Wyndham William Lewis's Heath Estate before arriving at the Rhymney Railway's Parade Station, just north of the TVR's Queen Street Station.

Not only did the Rhymney carry a substantial proportion of the coal tonnage handled at Bute Docks but it was also responsible for stimulating suburban development and providing long-term employment in the town's rural outskirts. After its passenger services were established people who worked in Cardiff saw the opportunity to build homes conveniently near to the railway in the countryside to the north of town and travel daily to work. At the opening of the twentieth century, Llanishen and Lisvane became fashionable dormitory villages mainly for well-off people working in Cardiff. The Heath was still open countryside but the company noted that houses were beginning to be built along Rhyd-y-pennau Road and the as yet unnamed Heathwood Road following the opening of a halt (Heath Low) in the

<hr />

[1] *Western Mail*, 11 May 1912; see also *Western Mail*, 29 Nov. 1980.

vicinity by the Cardiff Railway. In response, the Rhymney Railway built Heath (High Level) Halt in 1919 to take advantage of the added potential of passenger traffic. This second halt accelerated further building on these roads and also created a stimulus for wider suburban development on the Heath in the 1920s and early 1930s when large-scale house-building began in Heath Park Avenue, Heath Halt Road, Lake Road North, Heath Park Crescent and Crystal Avenue. Convenient rail travel to and from Cardiff was given prominence in the advertising campaigns run by the promoters of the large private estates on the Heath in the 1930s. 800,000 passengers a year used the Rhymney's Parade Station terminus at Cardiff before it was demolished in 1924.

The Cardiff Railway

This line roughly demarcates the present northern boundary of the Heath district. During the second half of the nineteenth century the disagreements between the third Marquess of Bute and the Taff Vale Railway grew into open hostility. In 1855 the marquess made plans to build his own railway up the Taff and Cynon valleys to Merthyr Tydfil and Aberdare in order to break the TVR's monopoly over the local coal trade. The TVR made immediate counter-plans to build a new dock at the mouth of the river Ely, west of Cardiff, in order to break the marquess's shipping monopoly at his docks. Both schemes were turned down by Parliament because of their potential to create such fundamental upheaval within the local economy.

Lord Bute was still intent on becoming a railway owner, however, because he believed that a railway would offer him a better return than his docks. In 1897 he submitted plans to build a watered-down version of his Taff valley railway; this time, its track would end at Pontypridd except for a few short local extensions. Significantly, however, he asked for permission to build a junction with the TVR at Treforest where that railway entered the Taff valley from the Rhondda. If Parliament had prevented Lord Bute from poaching coal traffic from the TVR in the valleys of the Taff and Cynon, they obviously believed in giving him the chance of trying his luck in the Rhondda Valley for they gave him permission to build his railway to Pontypridd, along with running rights from Treforest to the Rhondda Valley. It would be called the Cardiff Railway. As the *Cardiff Directory* for 1899 explained:

> In 1897 the Cardiff Railway Company obtained Parliamentary powers to construct a railway from the Bute Docks to Pontypridd and with junctions with the Taff Vale and Rhymney Railways establish a direct communication with the Rhondda, Aberdare, Merthyr and the Monmouthshire Valleys. This railway, principally intended for mineral and goods traffic, will be more immediately connected with the Roath Dock and the Deep Water Dock [i.e. what became Queen Alexandra Dock] now in process of formation.

Lord Bute was elated; at last he had broken into the railway business. He began work immediately, before the TVR could devise any counter-proposals. His financial prospects were blossoming for he would be in a position to compete for the coal trade of the Rhondda Valleys, now the most productive part of the coalfield.

The Cardiff Railway was originally planned to run up from Roath Dock via Roath and alongside the newly opened Roath Park before turning west to the Heath by a bridge under the Rhymney Railway embankment. As a temporary measure to reduce initial outlay on this leg of the route, however, Bute was given the right to run his trains up as far as the Heath on the Rhymney Railway. There, his new railway would branch off short of the Llanishen viaduct and run westwards as far as Tongwynlais where it would bear north into the coalfield via the Taff Vale. By 1907, although the third marquess had died in the meantime, tracks had been laid as far as Treforest.

But the new railway company had underestimated the TVR's resilience. Since 1902 they had been preparing to fight Cardiff Railway's plan to link up with their rails at Treforest. They had bought a narrow strip of land alongside their track, pretending that they needed it to lay down new sidings, and proceeded to use it as a legal barrier to prevent the Cardiff Railway from crossing over it to join their track. They also stubbornly rejected the siting of the proposed junction and all methods of constructing it shown on plans submitted to them over many years by the Cardiff Railway. By a combination of technical objections and delaying tactics they managed to keep up their defence until 1908.

Time and money were running out for the Cardiff Railway. They had spent a small fortune on legal action against the TVR, all to no avail, but worse still their shareholders were beginning to agitate for a return on their outlay. The Cardiff Railway had been the most expensive per mile to be built in the coalfield and at the end of ten years' effort no income was being generated. The TVR realised that the CR was in deep financial trouble and saw an opportunity to end the expensive wrangling between the two companies. It promised to construct the contentious junction at Treforest on condition that both companies agreed to a merger. Given their financial position, there was no alternative for the Cardiff company. They accepted the offer and parliamentary consent for the agreement was sought.

True to their word, the TVR immediately bridged the disputed strip of land bordering their railway with a low wooden platform, laid rails across it and installed the junction. As a gesture to convince all and sundry of the goodwill that existed between the two companies the TVR allowed a Cardiff Railway coal train to cross from one railway to another on 15 May 1908. It travelled from the Bute Colliery at Treherbert with the Marquess of Bute and TVR directors on board and after transferring from one railway to the other at Treforest it made its way down to Cardiff. The occasion was given wide publicity. A local newspaper was enthusiastic: 'The Marquess rode on his own engine to open up his new line with a train of coal from his own colliery loaded in his own wagons for shipment at his own docks'.

But the marquess's dreams were to turn to (coal) dust! Celebrations came to an untimely end when, in August 1908, the attempt to merge was rejected by Parliament

19 A northbound train leaving Heath Halt (Low) in 1919.

due to fierce opposition by dock and railway owners at Newport and Barry who feared the might of combined Bute and TVR interests and resources. The TVR dismantled the junction at Treforest and the ceremonial coal-train became the first and last train to achieve the transfer. Without the crucial route into the Rhondda Valleys the CR had lost its true purpose. The fourth marquess and his board of directors were left to lick their wounds.

The Cardiff Railway were now desperate for money. They hastened to open up their railway for passenger traffic between Pontypridd and Cardiff but this was a poor substitute for coal. The service began on 1 March 1911, but even though the company managed to augment it with a limited amount of goods traffic it still had to struggle for existence. Between 1914 and 1918 war-time restrictions forced the Taff Vale, Rhymney and Cardiff companies to pool their assets under a unified management. This was a step in the right direction for it succeeded in ending the hostility which had ravaged their resources for so many years. In 1921 Parliament formalised this alliance with an Act for the amalgamation of over 120 railway companies into four groups. Consequently, the independent railways of the South Wales coalfield were merged into an enlarged Great Western Railway Company.

The former Cardiff Railway line continued to struggle on but there was no appreciable demand for its services outside Cardiff; in 1931 it was closed between Coryton and Pontypridd. The 1930s, however, saw the emergence of extensive new housing suburbs on each side of its route through the north of Cardiff and demand for

20 Heath Halt (Low) in the early 1920s, looking towards Coryton.

passenger travel between Coryton, Whitchurch, Rhiwbina, the Heath and city centre increased. The approach to Heath Halt from the west had always been kept open by lane access to Heath Park Avenue (between Nos 88 and 90) and later extended (between Nos 87 and 89) into King George V Drive. In response to more frequent use the GWR improved the platforms at Rhiwbina and Heath halts, which had been installed in 1911, and opened a new halt at Birchgrove.

For thirty years, the Coryton Line, as it became known, provided an effective commuter service for the residents of north Cardiff, but in the 1960s the rapid development of road transport took its toll and in 1963 it was scheduled for closure by British Railways. Strong local opposition prevailed, however, and it remained in use after being reduced to a single track in 1966. During the 1980s its operation was facilitated by the introduction of the Countyride scheme by the local authority which provided financial aid to meet limited capital costs. In 1996 it reverted to private ownership when it was purchased by Prism Rail Company and now operates as one of the lines run by Cardiff Railways.

Urbanisation

During the second half of the nineteenth century Cardiff experienced an unprecedentedly rapid growth of population. More and more people became drawn to its thriving economy, based on the export trade from the coalfield. In 1851 its population numbered 18,351 but had risen to 164,333 by 1901, a dramatic eight-fold increase in fifty years. In 1875 Cardiff Corporation gained parliamentary assent to increase the area of the borough from 2,880 to 8,498 acres by adding largely undeveloped areas on the west bank of the Taff to the west and to the east of the existing built-up area on either side of Newport Road. This extension was followed by a period of rapid house-building on much of this land, which transformed the small clusters of houses at Grangetown, Canton and Roath into dense new suburbs. All this development was undertaken by private enterprise—principally a small group of landowners whose estates are considered in turn in this section—but was increasingly regulated by the Borough (later City) Council.

The Heath Estate

1880 was a significant date in the history of the Heath. It was about this time that the Marquess of Bute released part of the Cathays Estate for building. In a short time Cathays Terrace was laid out and its vicinity became the new suburb of Cathays. By about 1890, the tide of urbanisation extended northward as far as Whitchurch Road and, because Cardiff's population was still growing, continued residential development seemed inevitable.

The Heath Estate, built up by the Lewis family, of which some account was given earlier, lay immediately beyond Whitchurch Road. In September 1871 its owner, Wyndham William Lewis, died aged 44 without a male heir. Annie Mary, the only child of his first marriage, was then aged 20 years and Charlotte Eleanor, the only child of his second marriage, was to be born a week or so after her father's death. The Revd W.P. Lewis's will (1848) had stipulated that, if W.W. Lewis died without male issue, the Heath Estate would pass to his sister, Ann Price Lewis. In 1850 she had married George Thomas Clark, the former trustee and manager of the Dowlais Iron Company. In 1865 they had bought and settled at the remarkable Talygarn House in the Vale of Glamorgan; obviously, under these circumstances, they had no incentive to move to Heath House after inheriting it and they began to let it to tenants. By 1872 it was occupied by George W.G. Thomas, whose career and interests displayed similarities with those of Wyndham William Lewis. In 1860, at the early age of seventeen, he inherited the Rhymney Valley estate of Ystrad Mynach House when his father died. Following his education at Oxford, his involvement in county matters rapidly led to his appointment as a justice of the peace for the Caerphilly Division and a deputy lieutenant of Glamorgan. He served as High Sheriff in 1870, still aged only

27. He enjoyed hunting and kept a pack of harriers at Ystrad Mynach House. His refined manner, sympathetic nature and generosity made him well-liked but his singularity lay in his intense interest in farming. An impressive display of trophies in the dining room at The Heath testified to his outstanding success as a stock-breeder. Cattle and horses raised on his estate regularly gained prizes at prestigious shows. 'Gendarme', the most celebrated of his horses, won every available prize in its competition class before finally being sold to the King of Italy. After George Thomas's death in 1885 aged 42[1] his widow Ellen lived on at The Heath until 1893.

At G.T. Clark's death in 1898, the estate passed to his son, Godfrey Lewis Clark, and later, in 1918, to his grandson Wyndham Damer Clark, neither of whom had cause to live at The Heath, which continued to be occupied by tenants until the 1930s.

Shortly after W.W. Lewis's death a plot of land in the south-western corner of the Heath Estate was sold. It lay in the parish of Llandaff and people living in the Gabalfa area who were finding difficulty in making the roundabout journey to worship in the cathedral (in those days there was of course no bridge over the Taff on Western Avenue), sought to establish a chapel-of-ease on the eastern bank of the river. They appealed to the trustees of the estate for land and obtained an acre at the corner of North Road and Whitchurch Road, just south of the former Heath turnpike gate on North Road. The new chapel, dedicated to St Mark, was opened in 1876[2] and the following year a new parish of Gabalfa was created with St Mark's as its church.

By 1888 a strip of land alongside the Wedal Brook across the estate from Gabalfa had been leased to the Taff Vale Railway for the construction of their new branch line to carry coal to the Marquess of Bute's Roath Dock (opened in 1887) via a more easterly route through open land on the fringes of Cardiff. A train travelling to Roath Dock on the afternoon of 27 April 1905 arrived at its destination without a guard. Thomas Jones, who had been riding on top of the coal loaded into the end wagon, as was expected of guards in the days before brake-vans, was later found lying with severe head injuries at the side of the track near where it passed under the Rhymney Railway at Cathays Cemetery. He could not remember how or why he had fallen off the train. It was suggested at the official inquiry that he might have been knocked off by boys throwing stones from the bridge. Although this could not be proved to be the cause of the accident, the inspecting officer concluded that the practice of requiring guards to travel perched on loads in open wagons was too risky to be continued and strongly recommended that the Taff Vale should add brake-vans to all their trains. The company did not comply for some years but eventually the practice became universal on goods trains without continuous fitted brakes.[3]

The Roath Branch effectively isolated the south-eastern corner of the Heath Estate and during the last decade of the nineteenth century further detached portions at

---

[1] Obituaries were published in the *Western Mail*, 10 Dec. 1885, and *Cardiff Times*, 12 Dec. 1885.

[2] A full account appears in the *Cardiff Times*, 30 Sept. 1876.

[3] *Welsh Railway Archive*, i, no. 5 (May 1992).

Table 1
The Clark Family's Heath Estate: First Building Phase

	1899	*1909*	*1919*	*1929*	*1939*	*1949*	*1959*
Whitchurch Road	34	68	164	170	182	182	182
Allensbank Road west side	15	44	70	70	70	72	72
North Road east side	-	2	23	23	23	23	23
Allensbank Crescent	12	23	23	23	23	23	23
Talygarn Street	30	40	60	60	60	60	60
Manor Street	33	80	88	88	88	88	88
Llanishen Street	9	48	89	89	89	89	89
Inglefield Avenue			56	56	56	56	56
Borstal Avenue (renamed Summerfield Avenue 1929)			37	42	42	42	42
Edington Avenue			43	46	48	48	48
Soberton Avenue			31	31	39	39	39
Clodien Avenue			34	102	102	102	102
Banastre Avenue			11	14	14	14	14
Flaxland Avenue			8	42	42	42	42
Longspears Avenue				35	35	35	35
St Mark's Avenue				18	18	18	18
Sachville Avenue				-	-	-	-
Curll Avenue				-	-	-	-
Heath Park Avenue west side			34	41	59	62	62

Sources: Cardiff Directory; Electoral Registers.

Lisvane, Llanishen, Birchgrove and Cefn y Coed Farm (east of Roath Park Lake) were leased or sold for house-building. In 1896, W.W. Lewis's daughters sold 10 acres at The Mount and Lower Wedal to Cardiff Corporation which, along with a further 20 acres bought from Lord Tredegar, was used to extend Cathays Cemetery northwards of Wedal Brook (the section between Eastern Avenue and Heathwood Grove).

A letter written by Wyndham Damer Clark to Cardiff Corporation in March 1937 reveals his family's intentions at the end of the nineteenth century: '[My] predecessors in title, as you know, gave the corporation a considerable portion of land which now forms part of Roath Park and the land at the Heath has been retained with the idea of developing it as a residential area, for which it is eminently suitable'. So, during the 1890s, the estate was leasing land bordering its southern boundary for house-building along Whitchurch Road. As a result, a large portion of the main estate, comprising the lands of Allen's Bank Farm (demolished about 1911), became ripe for development because it was now within easy access of gas, water and sewerage. In February 1893 the 1,200-square yard corner site between Whitchurch Road and Allensbank Road was leased to the two brothers, J.B. and S.A. Brain, as the site of the Heath Hotel and three shops. The hotel was first licensed in August 1899 and the lease purchased in 1909. Table 1 shows that four new streets and a small park had also been laid out behind it by that time.

Table 1 also shows how building developed westwards and northwards, maintaining access to Allensbank Road and Whitchurch Road. The area was soon served by

21 Class 3, Allensbank School, in 1923.

Cardiff's electric tramway network, which was extended to Whitchurch Road during the first decade of the twentieth century. In 1900 the Forward Movement, working to expand membership of the Presbyterian Church of Wales, opened a hall to hold 400 opposite the Barracks Field on Whitchurch Road. The early years of its mission concentrated on preventing the prostitutes who frequented open ground bordering Maindy Barracks from establishing a permanent presence in the locality by taking up tenancies in the new houses which were being built along Whitchurch Road. The success of this campaign and the effects of the 1904 Religious Revival spurred the congregation to extend the church by adding a new hall in 1906 to hold 850 people. An article on the church in the *Cardiff and South Wales Advertiser* in February 1921 noted that 'Just over 20 years ago a mission of the Forward Movement was established here and today there is a fine church with a membership of nearly 600 and a Sunday School of nearly 1,000. Remarkable figures for 20 years' growth'.

In November 1906 local residents, led by members of Crwys Road Methodist Church, set up the Heath Wesleyan Mission in a purpose-built meeting-house at 77 Allensbank Road, at the corner of Manor Street. Their circuit magazine reveals that they were promoting a lively cause and were, by December 1910, fostering hopes of expansion in the area. Their plans apparently failed to materialise and there seem to be no references to Heath Mission after 1920. The ground floor of No 77 was converted into Burn & Prior's motor garage after 1922.

The building of Allensbank School in Llanishen Street in 1904, with proposed provision for 1,200 pupils, suggests that further development in the area was expected. In order to combat an unusually virulent strain of diphtheria in children, the school was destined to become one of three in Cardiff to pioneer immunisation of pupils against the disease in 1926.[1]

Houses were built in terraces in accordance with prevailing practice but in a variety of styles and a mixture of brick or stone elevations. Roofs were pantiled or slated and all houses and roads were paved and lit by gas. Most building activity here ceased in 1914 with the outbreak of war but construction work in some streets was resumed after 1918.

A variety of shops soon began to appear in houses along Whitchurch Road and local tradesmen took advantage of some undeveloped plots to establish businesses there: Thresher's coal and haulage yard in Whitchurch Road and Lattey's builder's yard in Allensbank Road are two examples. Other empty plots had a more chequered history. The 1900 Ordnance Survey map shows what appears to be a stable block on a triangle of land behind 3 Talygarn Street, which by 1913 had been partitioned into Thurbon's smithy, Hewett's builder's yard and Dray's bakery. The smithy was converted into the Ensign Garage in 1922 and the bakery closed in 1924, when the garage became Hewett's, which survived until the Second World War. After 1945 the bakery was reopened by Thomas Richards but the vacant garage and yard were not occupied until 1950, when they were acquired by Associated Clay Industries Ltd, a bathroom-ware company. They were later bought by J.P. McDougall & Co. Ltd, decorators' merchants. Since 1975 the old bakery has been occupied by a firm of furniture restorers trading as Back to the Wood.

A strong community spirit was already growing in this emerging suburb. The Heath, Cardiff, United Choral Society had been formed by 1920, with Sidney C. Roberts as its honorary secretary. Its second annual concert was held in the Cory Hall in the city centre on 23 February 1921, when members, accompanied by four guest artistes, performed a programme which included selections from Gounod's 'Faust'.[2] St Mark's Church Institute at the Gabalfa end of Whitchurch Road was licensed for dancing during the early 1920s; by 1927 Warwick Hall had been built off Banastre Avenue near its junction with the middle section of Whitchurch Road. A variety of social activities were held in the hall's ground floor assembly room whilst regular dance sessions accompanied by a resident band along with an associated school of dance were conducted in its first-floor ballroom. Its entertainment licence was kept up until the outbreak of war in 1939, when it was taken over by the Army, but it was not renewed after the war when the building came to be used for other purposes. In November 1945 the city council granted permission to change its use to a dental laboratory and in the Cardiff directories for 1952 and 1955 it is described as Warwick

---

[1] *Annual Report of the Medical Officer of Health, Cardiff* (1926).

[2] *Cardiff and South Wales Advertiser*, Feb. 1921.

22 Church elders in front of Curll Avenue Gospel Hall. *Standing at rear (left to right:* W.J. Armer, John Parkin, Robert Loosemore; *middle row:* Fred Goaman, Alf Pitman, Frank Dobson, Charles Carr, Bert Goaman; *seated:* Sam Crosby, William Doble, William Armer, — Goaman.

Hall Works, occupied by Rotary & Percussive Tools Ltd, a firm of precision engineers. It is currently a complex of studios devoted to recording music and the expression of practical arts such as painting, sculpting and pottery.

In June 1920 the Congregationalists held their first service locally in a converted Army hut off Sachville Avenue and by 1939 membership had increased sufficiently for them to open a permanent brick building on the site. Worship came to an end here in July 1986 and the premises now serve as the headquarters of the Welsh Association of Youth Clubs. During 1915 an offshoot group from Mackintosh Gospel Hall began meeting in a shop in Whitchurch Road as a temporary measure. Within a few years they had grown in numbers sufficient to warrant the building of their own premises in nearby Curll Avenue. Construction was undertaken by the members themselves and they succeeded in opening their new church on Boxing Day 1921.

The Taff Vale Railway's Roath Dock branch attracted some industrial activity. A private siding, called Lattey's Siding,[1] which probably served Norman Lattey's building and contracting yard further down Allensbank Road, was laid about 1902 near the bridge under Allensbank Road. By 1907 it had become known as Strachan's

[1] R.A. Cooke, *Atlas of the Great Western Railway as at 1947* (1988), map 174.

Siding[1] after it came to serve a railway engineering works which John Strachan, the successful Cardiff contractor, built alongside it. The works are referred to in the *Cardiff Directory* for 1910 but by then it had already changed hands. An advertisement in the *Western Mail* for 9 July 1909 refers to the sale of leasehold premises known as Allensbank Works, along with plant and machinery, on the instructions of Strachan's executors. It was bought by the Flottmann Engineering Co. Ltd, a German-owned firm specialising in high quality drilling equipment for the mining industry. They retained the premises, apart from two periods of confiscation by the government during the two World Wars, until about 1960. In 1962 the building was purchased by F.W. Morgan Ltd, timber merchants, and was occupied by them until it was acquired by its present owners, Brittons Building Supplies Ltd, in 1994.

All the street names in the area illustrate the connection with the Heath Estate. G.T. Clark, an accomplished historian who in 1886 published *Limbus Patrum Morganiae et Glamorganiae*, recording the genealogies of the leading families of Glamorgan, was proudly aware of his wife's descent from the Welsh princes who had ruled east Glamorgan before its subjection by the Normans at the end of the eleventh century. Despite the Norman occupation her family had maintained their influence, which centred on their ancestral home at the Van, Caerphilly. Clark gives due preference to the Lewis family of the Van in his book, who supply several street names in the Heath. In the early seventeenth century, Sir Edward Lewis of the Van married Lady Ann Sachville, heiress of the family who lived at Edington Manor (Wilts.). In the late seventeenth century William Lewis of the Van married Margaret, heiress of Lawrence Banastre of Boarstall Tower (Bucks.) (Borstal Avenue had been renamed Summerfield Avenue by 1929). In the eighteenth century Thomas Lewis of the Van married Ann Marie Curll, heiress of Walter Curll of Soberton House (Hants.). Among the properties inherited by Thomas Lewis were Longspears, Flaxland and Inglefield manors. Manor Street makes direct reference to the manorial background of the Lewis family and Talygarn Street is a reminder that Ann Price Clark and her husband were then living in Talygarn House.

House-owners in the north-eastern corner of the Heath had enjoyed the benefits of rail travel to and from Cardiff ever since Heath Halt (Low) on the Cardiff Railway was opened in March 1911. Godfrey Clark, who was chairman of the Rhymney Railway, realised that this advantage would lead to a demand for further houses near the new station and immediately drained and leased 30 plots of land on the western side of Heath Park Avenue, between Allensbank Road and Heath Halt Road, to George Paltridge, an experienced master-builder. By 1918 (the year Clark died) a complete development of 34 good quality houses had been constructed on this site. By October 1919 the company was convinced of the wisdom of opening a similar halt on their own railway, which came to be called Heath Halt (High). After that date, house-owners in Heath Park Avenue, Heath Park Crescent, Heath Halt Road and

---

[1] G.A. Sekon, 'Cardiff: the City, its Railways and Commerce', *Railway Magazine*, xx (1907).

23 The Heath in 1920, just before large-scale house-building began.

24 Before road improvements began: Mr and Mrs Porter stand in their market garden alongside Caerphilly Road in 1910. The New Inn is visible behind them.

Heathwood Road were able to travel either by road or by one of two railways.

Cardiff's population continued to grow as the nineteenth century came to a close and the corporation once again made repeated, though unsuccessful, attempts to secure another boundary extension in 1889, 1898, 1900 and 1910. In 1922, however, it was given power to incorporate parts of the parishes of Caerau, Michaelston-super-Ely, Llandaff, Whitchurch, Llanishen and Llanedeyrn, an area totalling 5,500 acres with a population of 19,000. The city was now able to embark on its own extensive house-building projects on some of the land acquired to the west. To the north, it opted to encourage private building projects which were already well in hand on the Heath by advancing money on mortages over twenty years at 5 per cent. This scheme was launched in the Heath in 1924 and the sums borrowed varied from £1,300 to £1,600.

At this date the Heath was still a largely rural area: roads were narrow and poorly surfaced, there was no electricity supply, water was obtained from wells and household waste was drained into private cesspits. If developers were to be attracted to the area the corporation would have to install vital services. It wasted no time in getting to work. Its priority was to improve communication: access roads were widened, properly surfaced and drained, and provided with kerbs and pavements. All bridges over or under them were widened and strengthened. Water and gas mains, sewers and electricity and telephone cables were laid as the work progressed. These improvements extended northwards along Allensbank Road, North Road and

Caerphilly Road, then laterally along Heathwood Road and Tŷ Glas Road. House-building along these arterial roads accelerated as services became available and travel for the new residents became easier.

Once the council had installed essential services along the improved access roads of the Heath, developments were possible on the remainder of the estate. As the first phase of building in the lower corner was drawing to a close, plans were prepared for a second phase of development in the north-western corner. Terraced housing was built on the Clark family's land along North Road between St Mark's church and the lodge at the old gateway to Heath House, opposite the Cross Inn, before the First World War. During the 1920s this ribbon development was extended as a row of semi-detached houses as far as the Birchgrove crossroads and for some distance up the south side of Heathwood Road. The estate's second main phase of building consisted of an integrated residential project on the land behind this fringe of housing (bounded by the present-day St Anthony Road to the east). Streets would focus on a wide central avenue running east from Caerphilly Road which would provide access and services to the whole development. This was to be named Van Avenue to commemorate the Lewis family's ancestral home near Caerphilly but by the time the plans were approved by the council in 1929 its name had been changed to Rhydhelig Avenue. Building began in the early 1930s (see Table 2).

The first houses were constructed in terraces of between four and eight. Later houses were built in pairs, usually with a grassed forecourt embellished with wrought-

25 Mrs Porter outside her cottage, supervising delivery of produce. Her gate opened on to Caerphilly Road.

Table 2
The Clark Family's Heath Estate: Second Building Phase

	1899	1909	1919	1929	1939	1949	1959
Caerphilly Road east side				39	45	45	45
Heathwood Road south side				8	60	110	127
Allensbank Road north of Eastern Avenue			11	41	50	50	62
Rhydhelig Avenue					67	79	79
St George's Road					15	15	15
St Helen's Road					42	42	42
St Agnes Road					46	46	46
St Alban Avenue					44	44	44
St Aidan Crescent					21	21	21
St Augustine Road					41	41	48
St Ambrose Road					7	39	64
St Anthony Road						4	104
St Benedict Crescent							68
St Agatha Road							48
St Angela Road							56
Heath Park Lane							40
King George V Drive							225

Sources: Cardiff Directory; Electoral Registers. *Notes:* Figures are Caerphilly Road and Heathwood Road are approximate only. King George V Drive was developed after Cardiff Corporation purchased the Clark Estate.

iron railings of standard design set upon a low brick wall. A greater emphasis on space gave the opportunity to provide a driveway and sometimes a garage. All the houses were constructed in brick, had slated roofs and were universally supplied with gas and electricity. Street names took up the 'Saint' prefix which has become such a distinguishing feature of the area today and reflects the Clark family's deep interest in history, with special emphasis here on the early church.

As this second building phase got under way the Heath Estate revealed plans for a third phase of development intended to occupy the land between the first two schemes. They were first submitted to the council in November 1924 and given final approval in January 1934. This major development would extend across the middle of the Heath Estate from North Road to Allensbank Road and a number of open-ended streets off today's North Road, Whitchurch Road and Allensbank Road show how it was proposed to integrate its access with the existing developments that surrounded it. Rose Mount Place, Longspears Avenue, Flaxland Avenue, Curll Avenue, Sachville Avenue, Banastre Avenue, Soberton Avenue and Summerfield Avenue, along with two road entrances in Allensbank Road (the former, between Nos 177 and 179, is now occupied by a garage and lane, and the latter, between Nos 205 and 207, is now a link road with King George V Drive) are all unfinished streets originally planned to give access to this third phase of development. For example, 'Proposed Road Number 30' on the town planning scheme for the Heath was a continuation of Flaxland Avenue over the Roath Dock branch railway to a junction with the eastern end of Rhydhelig Avenue, then onward on roughly the same alignment as today's St Anthony Road and

Heathway and under the Cardiff Railway to a junction with Tŷ Glas Road in Llanishen. An unused stone-arched bridge under the railway can still be seen a hundred yards or so east of Tŷ Glas Station.

This third building phase never materialised. In 1937 the corporation opened negotiations to buy a strip of land extending across the Heath Estate in order to extend Western Avenue eastward from Gabalfa. This would cut a 69-acre swathe through the heart of the proposed new development broad enough to accommodate a 120 ft dual carriageway and slip-roads. The corporation overcame deadlocked negotiations over the price of the land by offering to purchase the whole of the remainder of the estate from the Clark family. It was becoming increasingly unprofitable to lease land for development because its price had been falling steadily since the First World War. This may have influenced Wyndham Damer Clark's decision to sell Heath House and all the undeveloped remainder of the estate, amounting to 203 acres, to the council for £105,000. The sale was completed in January 1938. It marks the end of the Lewis family's connection with the Heath. Soon, the war halted all building on the second phase of the earlier development (Rhydhelig Avenue) and was not resumed for another ten years. The development was finally completed in the late 1950s.

The New House Estate

In 1869, two years before his death, Wyndham William Lewis bought New House, his father's childhood home, along with 450 acres of land in the parishes of Whitchurch and Llanishen, from his widowed aunt for £12,900. Annie Mary, his only child, was 20 at his death. The provisions of the Revd W.P. Lewis's will precluded her from inheriting Heath House after her father's days but W.W. Lewis's actions in purchasing land and property in addition to the estate bequeathed to him by his uncle ensured that Annie Mary and her future half-sister, Charlotte Eleanor, would not be deprived of an inheritance after their father's death. There is no evidence, however, that Annie Mary went to live at New House. She is as described as living in Hatfield (Herts.) in 1874 and 1886 and in London in 1887, 1899 and 1904. Her half-sister Charlotte moved to live first in Dunbartonshire, when her mother, Maud, married her second husband, William Orr Ewing of Rhu Lodge, and then to St Boswells, where she met and married Col. Murray-Threipland of Fingask and Toftingall in 1899. After her marriage, she and her husband made their home at New House and their son, Patrick Murray-Threipland, was born there in 1905. Dryburgh Avenue and Toftingall Avenue, two streets laid out on New House land west of Caerphilly Road, reflect Col. Murray-Threipland's estates in Roxburgh and Caithness.

The New House Estate owned all the land east of the Ton-yr-ywen Brook and immediately north of Heathwood Road in the 1930s. It comprised the 157 acres of racecourse ground bought for £3,100 from Cardiff Corporation by W.W. Lewis in 1849 and, because it had not been inherited by him under the terms of his uncle's will, was available for him to bequeath to his daughters.

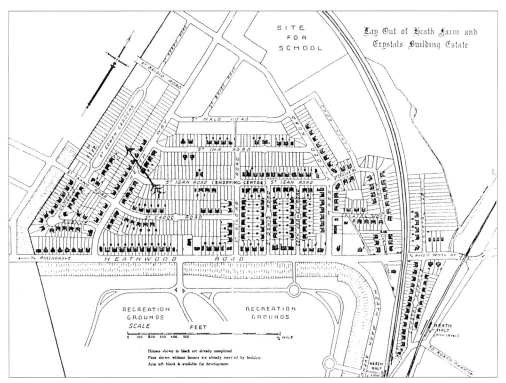

26 Layout of the Heath Farm and Crystals Building Estate, 1938, showing the proposed development of the land bought by W.W. Lewis in 1849 (see Plate 12).

By the 1880s and 1890s house-building on the Lewis Estate in Llanishen village had already begun and this was continued by the Murray-Threipland family during the early decades of the twentieth century. In the 1930s they turned their attention to that part of their estate which bordered Heathwood Road. In 1930 Col. Murray-Threipland sold a long strip of New House land to the council to enable it to widen and install services in that road. In 1932, his son Patrick Murray-Threipland managed to persuade the council to change the zoning of the Crystals area in its town planning scheme from industrial to residential use. These two critical measures paved the way for the immediate development of the New House Estate north of Heathwood Road. Crystal Avenue, Cefn Carnau Road and lower Maes-y-coed Road had been laid out by the mid 1930s. In 1934 Patrick Murray-Threipland gained approval for a major project, in excess of 100 acres, to develop Heath Farm and the Crystals. The farm lay alongside Heathwood Road beneath the site of the present Heathwood Court: its boundary wall can be seen fronting the houses between Heathwood Court and St Gildas Road. The plan (Plate 26) from a New House Estate promotional brochure shows how building had progressed by late 1938 or early 1939. Heath Farm is shown on this map but it was later demolished to make way for the development. The objectives of Cardiff's town planning scheme are boldly reflected in the brochure:

27 An aerial photograph of 1937 showing house-building getting underway on the New House Estate to the north of Heathwood Road, on the lines shown in the plan reproduced in Plate 26.

HEATH FARM AND CRYSTALS BUILDING ESTATE

Combined with the advantages of living in the country, it is quickly and easily accessible to all parts of the City by excellent train and bus services. Almost every house commands a view of the Glamorgan Hills to the North, yet within five minutes the centre of the City can be reached

The streets, mostly named after Welsh Saints, are well laid out in accordance with the Cardiff Corporation Town Planning Scheme; there is a convenient shopping centre, a site nearby reserved by the Corporation for a Secondary School, and there will be public gardens and ground suitable for tennis courts.

Some street names are connected with the Lewis family. Cefn Carnau Road commemorates the Cefn Carnau lands inherited by Thomas Lewis when he married Elizabeth Thomas and then built New House as their family home in the mid eighteenth century. Aberpergwm Road, renamed St Denis Road by 1939, originally commemorated the ancestral home of Charlotte Murray-Threipland's mother at

Table 3

The Murray-Threipland Family's New House Estate: Heath Farm and Crystals Land

	1899	*1909*	*1919*	*1929*	*1939*	*1949*	*1959*
Heathwood Road				6	56	74	92
Crystal Avenue					44	44	44
Cefn Carnau Road					26	26	26
Maes-y-coed Road					38	49	111
Aberpergwm Road					23	23	23
Crystal Wood Road					27	38	48
St Cenydd Road					10	10	10
Crystal Rise					14	14	14
Heathway					45	70	85
St Isan Road					44	62	90
St Gildas Road					22	22	22
St Cadog Road					10	34	54
St Tanwg Road					3	12	12
St Govan Road					32	42	42
St Ina Road					14	70	73
St Edwen Gardens					2	42	58
Crystal Glen						20	27
St Malo Road						11	47
St Brioc Road						3	25
St Brigid Road							17
St Asaph Close							20

Sources: Cardiff Directory; Electoral Registers. *Notes:* Figures for Heathwood Road (north side between Ton-yr-ywen Avenue and Three Arches Bridge) are approximate only. Aberpergwm Road was renamed St Denis Road in 1939. In the 1980s, after the Heath Farm land had been purchased by Cardiff Corporation, 25 houses were built at Eton Court.

Aberpergwm House in the Vale of Neath. Maes-y-coed Road and other roads bearing the prefix 'Crystal' reflect their location at or near the former 40-acre Crystal Wood planted by the Lewis family in order to preserve game.

When war broke out in 1939, building on the New House Estate was abandoned and individual plots which had been reserved as house-sites were turned into allotment gardens. Most of the distinctive wrought-iron gates and railings which gave character to the houses which had already been built by this time were removed for scrap for the war effort. The map in the estate brochure shows roughly how far development had proceeded when interrupted by hostilities. Work on the unfinished half of the Heath Farm Estate was resumed after building restrictions were lifted at the end of the war and after planning consent for it (which had expired during the war) was renewed by the council in September 1948. Slight differences between pre-war and post-war building features can be noticed. Generally speaking, the slate roofs, gabled sash windows and wrought-iron railings of the pre-1939 houses were replaced by tiled roofs, non-gabled casement windows and low brick wall frontages in the newer houses. Table 3 gives a broad picture of the completed Heath Farm and Crystals Building Estate.

No houses had been planned for the land lying between Maes-y-coed Road and the railway to Coryton but a factory had been built at its western extremity, off Caerphilly Road, in 1931. It was set up by D. Morgan Rees & Sons for the manufacture of wire rope. This venture marked the revival of the renowned Excelsior wire-rope works, which the Rees family had established in Maindy at the turn of the century.[1] It was merged with British Ropes in 1926 but younger members of the family felt confident enough in 1931 that the business could make a fresh start on its own at the new site on Caerphilly Road. Its chief customer, however, was the coal industry and the company soon found itself facing a shrinking market as the South Wales coalfield declined after 1920. The company later re-amalgamated with British Ropes. Before the Caerphilly Road works closed in 1962 the National Museum of Wales photographed the complete process of manufacturing wire-rope, including the traditional method employed there of drawing the wire. The building was occupied by Ryan Plant Ltd, a plant-hire firm, from 1967 to 1975, when it became known as the Grove Works. It was later occupied by D.M. Builders Ltd but is now owned by Memory Lane bakeries and is awaiting demolition.

In 1938 the New House Estate brochure declared that much of the land between Maes-y-coed Road and the railway was 'reserved for the immediate building of a secondary school on Heath Farm by the Corporation'. This project was postponed on the outbreak of war and the land later became the 10-acre site for Ton-yr-ywen Primary School, opened in June 1952. The prefabricated dual-purpose building dates from the anxious years of the Cold War: wide doors and corridors would have allowed its rapid transformation into a hospital in the event of war. Classrooms still contain lockers which would have been used by patients. The school's catchment area today extends from Heath Park Avenue to Beulah Road.

In 1947 the council zoned the undeveloped land between the proposed primary school and the wire-rope factory as land to be put to any commercial or industrial use which would not affect the neighbourhood adversely. Maes-y-coed Road was completed from the school entrance to the newly demolished Ton-yr-ywen farmhouse on Caerphilly Road and a number of factories were set up along it. The site of the farmhouse was used for the Gnome photographic equipment factory, established by Heinrich Loebstein, a German Jew who owned a small factory manufacturing enlargers for processing film using sub-miniature cameras, who fled from Germany in 1938. He was persuaded by the goverment to set up a similar business on the Treforest Trading Estate, but soon had to abandon his premises when they were requisitioned by the War Office. He managed to secure another building in the centre of Cardiff, where he was requested to concentrate on making enlargers for use in aerial reconnaissance by the RAF. Business flourished to such an extent as to warrant a move to larger premises on the Heath at the end of the war, where the company went on to capture 80 per cent of the home market in its specialised products.[2] The firm took the 'Gnome' title from the brand name of one of its early enlargers and the factory soon came to be known as Gnome Corner. The factory closed in 1988 and the building was demolished in the early 1990s. In 1999 a supermarket belonging to the

[1] *Cardiff Spectator*, ii (no. 11).

[2] Ibid., ii (no. 10).

28 The four post-war factories clustered together at 'Gnome Corner', the junction of Caerphilly Road with Maes-y-coed Road.

Lidl chain was built on the site.

Also in 1947 a small footwear factory was built next to the Gnome site by Marcus Shoes Ltd, but by 1952 it had been taken over by Ilona Shoes, Cardiff, Ltd, who operated from Clifton Street. The factory had ceased production by 1955, when the rear of the building had been taken over as a distribution depot for Brooke Bond and Oxo, while C. & T. Harris (Calne) Ltd and Highbridge Bacon Co. Ltd, two bacon-curing firms, had moved into the main premises. In 1972 they were joined by Marsh & Baxter Ltd, when Brooke Bond moved to a small factory run by BEB Brushes (currently occupied by Heath Tyres Ltd). By 1977 all three bacon processors had vacated the former shoe factory, which was acquired by the present owners, L. Rossi & Son Ltd, ice-cream manufacturers, the following year.

A second boot and shoe factory was built adjoining the Ilona site in 1947 by F.G. Wigley & Co. Ltd of Mill Lane, Cardiff, who maintained production at the Heath site for about ten years. The building was purchased in September 1959 by Spillers Ltd, who reopened it as the Wonder Bakery, named after the family-run Wonder Cakes firm of Abertillery which they had recently acquired. The name was changed to Memory Lane in 1975. In 1980 the business was taken over by Dalgety Ltd, who

29 A group of distinguished visitors, including the Lord Mayor of Cardiff, to the Hopkinson Electric Co. factory in 1951. The precise occasion has not been identified.

carried out substantial developments at the bakery. In 1984, with the aid of a £500,000 government grant, they extended the site with the purchase of an adjoining 5-acre plot (owned by the former wire-rope firm) and added new buildings. They also took over in 1978 the adjoining building and plumbing warehouse set up by D. Morgan Edwards Ltd in 1968 and later owned by Sankey Ltd.[1] Memory Lane was acquired by the Grand Metropolitan Group in 1990 but reverted to independent ownership in 1997.

1947 also saw the establishment of a large factory on a 23-acre site on Maes-y-coed Road opposite the junction with Ton-yr-ywen Avenue by the Hopkinson Electric Co., which operated factories on a number of dispersed sites in London but at the end of the war wished to combine at a single location. Attracted to a Development Area by the grants available, the company planned a major project which aimed to employ 3,000 people on 500,000 square feet making electric motors for industry. Initial prospects were very promising: the plant turned out over a thousand motors a week by the end of its first year of production with only 900 employees and only half the

---

[1] *Western Mail*, 1 Oct. 1984 (advertising feature).

building completed.[1] Due to capital expenditure cuts, however, development was curtailed and production ceased in 1954. By 1963 the building had been acquired by the guided missiles division of the British Aircraft Corporation, before being taken over by Bristol Siddeley Engines Ltd by 1967. In 1972 the plant was bought by Merrett's Bakeries Ltd, who now operate within the Allied Bakeries Group.

By 1951 the newly established Welsh Regional Hospitals Board had set up its architect and surveyor's department in a new building adjoining the Hopkinson factory, where a number of hospital schemes throughout Wales were planned. By 1962 the department had moved to the city centre and the building became vacant. By about 1970 it had been acquired by the Post Office to house a new computer system intended to be used for billing customers. It later became a British Telecom building, closed in 1994, and in 2001 is awaiting development.

During the early 1970s land between the Post Office building and Ton-yr-ywen primary school began to be developed. In 1974 Marlborough Textiles Ltd set up a large warehouse there named Emeralda, intended as an outlet for their clothing factory in Roath. By 1986 the company had moved to east Cardiff and the Maes-y-coed Road building remained unused until 1993, when its current occupiers, Tesco Stores Ltd, secured it for a head office and renamed it Tesco House.

Development of the land behind the Emeralda warehouse began with three buildings designed to house a complex of business units. The first, containing three large units, was put up in about 1980, adjoining the school at the end of a new access road named Fieldway. The second, again containing three large units, was built in the late 1980s. In 1990 a third building, containing nine smaller units, was put up between the first two. Two other buildings were also constructed at this time. One was built as a head office by Knox & Wells Ltd, the long-established Cardiff builders. In 1990 they built and moved into an adjacent block, which they named Creswell House, while Norwest Holst (Construction) Ltd set up their head office in the first building, which they named Holst House. In 1996 Holst House was acquired by Thomas Graham, a firm of solicitors, and renamed St Ina House. There have been changes of tenancy in the business units, although some firms, such as British Telecom, Budd Electrical and Knox & Wells, have maintained a presence there for ten years or more.

An 8½-acre site east of Ton-yr-ywen school was bought by the city council for leisure and recreation and has been provided with a timber-built pavilion, with access from St Cenydd Road. Part of the land was used to build 25 houses, named Eton Court, in the early 1980s and provided with independent access from Maes-y-coed Road. By then the Murray-Threipland family, having disposed of its land to Cefn Estates and the B.P. Pension Fund, had moved away from Cardiff.

[1] *Industrial Wales*, no. 4 (June 1948).

The Bute Estate

In the early nineteenth century the second Marquess of Bute owned a wide swathe of territory east of the Lewis family's Heath Estate. In 1841 Lord Bute donated land on his Celyn farm to the Jewish community in Cardiff as a burial ground with access from Allensbank Road via Highfield Road. Prior to this, Jews were obliged to ship corpses to Bristol for interment. An inscription on the wall near the entrance reads:

> This Ground was given for a
> JEWS CEMETERY
> by the Most Noble
> John, Marquess of Bute
> A.D. 1841   A.M. 5602
> Mark Marks, President
> Solomon Marks, Treasurer
> Samuel Marks, Secretary

In the mid 1850s Cardiff Corporation bought over 100 acres of land in the south-eastern corner of the former Great Heath from the third marquess and other landowners, including Wyndham William Lewis of the Heath, in order to provide Cardiff with its own municipal burial ground. In 1859 a large new cemetery was opened there on land bounded by Allensbank Road, the Wedal Brook and Fairoak Road. In 1886 the corporation again bought land on the eastern fringe of the Heath from the third marquess, this time for the construction of the Heath Filter Beds (in the angle of Allensbank Road and Highfield Road) which were needed to purify water from their reservoir at Llanishen.

Private house-building began on the Bute lands of Rhyd-y-pennau, Celyn and Cefn y Coed farms near the Cardiff Railway and Rhymney Railway shortly before the First World War. People realised that they could enjoy the benefits of living in a pleasant rural environment and yet still be within quick and easy reach of the city after Heath Halt (Low) opened in 1911, followed by Heath Halt (High) in 1919. Although numbers of occupied houses on Heathwood Road in 1919 have not been obtained, it appears that some houses had been built there, along with others in Heath Park Avenue, by that date.

In 1924 worshippers who had moved to live in the new housing developments near the Heath railway halts began directing their energies towards establishing a local meeting-house. Their aspirations had been fired by a member of the Forward Movement Congregation at Heath Hall in Whitchurch Road who, under the influence of a vivid dream, convinced fellow members that a new church would soon stand at Rhyd-y-pennau Crossroads. Campaigners realised that the crossroads would provide a central gathering point within the new community and so they bought the reclaimed site of the former Bute Brickworks clay-pit at the junction of Rhyd-y-pennau Road and Llandennis Road, where they built a church to accommodate 300 people. The new

Table 4
The Bute Estate: Celyn and Cefn-y-Coed Farm Lands

	1899	*1909*	*1919*	*1929*	*1939*	*1949*	*1959*
Heathwood Road east of the Three Arches Bridge				12	18	20	20
Heath Park Avenue east side				41	59	62	62
Heath Park Crescent				8	8	8	8
Heath Halt Road				4	4	8	8
Highfield Road				7	7	7	7
Heathwood Grove					42	42	42
Allensbank Road east side	1	1	1	1	11	11	11

Sources: Cardiff Directory; Electoral Registers. *Notes:* Figures for Heathwood Road and Heath Park Avenue are approximate only. In the 1980s 129 houses and flats were built at Heath Mead and 88 at Heath Park Drive.

Park End Presbyterian Church was opened in January 1925.[1] Plans to extend the building were hampered by the Depression of the 1930s and the Second World War, during which the congregation's resources were redirected towards vital relief work, both at home and abroad. It was not until March 1966, when the large church building complex was opened, that their forty-year-old ambitions were fulfilled. Further improvements to the premises were carried out in January 2000.[2]

As noted earlier, today's Heath Halt Road and Heath Park Avenue had been brought up to standard by the Marquess of Bute in 1823 at the request of the Llanishen parish vestry. House-building along those roads and Heathwood Road accelerated during the 1920s and prompted the creation of new roads in the vicinity. Table 4 gives a general picture of development in this area, showing that this phase of development had come to an end by 1939.

In the mid 1980s two small-scale but significant residential developments took place on this eastern fringe of the Heath. At Heath Mead, land purchased by the corporation from Lord Bute in order to install the Heath Filter Beds became available for development when the purification plant became obsolete. This was used to build the Highfield Resource Centre, a local authority venture attended by people with disabilities engaged in producing craftware, printwork and an increasing variety of services for commercial purposes, and also to build 129 houses, some of which are reserved for people with disabilities.[3] At Heath Park Drive, land owned by Lord Bute and used by him to build his Cardiff Railway had been acquired by British Rail. It became available for a layout of 188 houses and flats when Heath railway junction was relocated a quarter of a mile northwards along the Rhymney Railway and when

[1] *Western Mail*, 5 Jan. 1925.

[2] G.N. Williams, *These Fifty Years* (1975); D. Robbins, *Park End at 60* (1985).

[3] *South Wales Echo*, 28 June 1985.

the southern part of the site was vacated in 1984 by the removal of Whitchurch & District Model Engineering Society's miniature railway circuit to its present location in Heath Park, where it re-opened in 1987.

Away on the western fringe of the New House Estate, Ton-yr-ywen farmland alongside Caerphilly Road, corresponding to the lots purchased by John Goodrich at the time of enclosure, also belonged to the Bute family. The house stood on a site later occupied by the Gnome photographic products factory: the old farmyard wall can be seen alongside the pavement on Caerphilly Road north of its junction with Maes-y-coed Road. The farm's land lay between Caerphilly Road and the Ton-yr-ywen Brook as far south as Heathwood Road.

In 1922 the Bute family transferred the administration of its South Wales estates to a private company named Mountjoy Ltd. As soon as the council had installed essential services in Caerphilly Road, the company began building houses, mostly in terraces of five, along its eastern flank from Heathwood Road to Maes-y-coed Road. Seven gaps were left at fairly regular intervals between these houses to accommodate access roads to a major housing development scheme which Mountjoy was proposing for all the Ton-yr-ywen farmland which lay behind them. This ambitious project began in 1930 at the Heathwood Road end of the estate where its corner lay diagonally over the crossroads from the newly rebuilt Birchgrove Inn.

Developments had been taking place at the Birchgrove crossroads for quite some time. A board school, originally known as Heath School, Whitchurch (now Birchgrove School), had been opened in 1897 close to a nucleus of early housing on Pant Bach

30 The rebuilding of the Birchgrove Inn in 1928. An unremarkable Victorian street-corner pub gives way to the bold and well-detailed building by Percy Thomas that stands on the site today.

31 The British Oxygen Company's factory on Maes-y-coed Road in 1967.

Road, Caerphilly Road and Birchgrove Road. A group of Wesleyan Methodists, who had long worshipped at the junction of Beulah Road and Caerphilly Road, built a hall on a site lower down Caerphilly Road at its junction with Coronation Road in 1903, to which they added a converted Army hut in 1921 to use as a Sunday school. In 1956 these premises were extended and modernised to become St Andrew's Church.

Mountjoy built a new street roughly parallel with Caerphilly Road along the eastern boundary of the estate from Heathwood Road to Maes-y-coed Road and named it Ton-yr-ywen Avenue. Three cross-streets linked it with the three lower access gaps between the Caerphilly Road houses, and these streets were appropriately called Tair Erw Road, Pedair Erw Road and Pum Erw Road (i.e. Three Acre Road, Four Acre Road and Five Acre Road) because they were built on fields bearing those names[1] (see Table 5).

An attractively laid out open area named Llwynfedw Gardens, which was completely in tune with the ideals of Cardiff's pre-war town planning scheme, formed

[1] See the tithe map of Whitchurch parish (1840) in the Glamorgan Record Office.

Table 5
The Bute Estate: Tony-yr-ywen Farm Land

	1899	*1909*	*1919*	*1929*	*1939*	*1949*	*1959*
Caerphilly Road east side		4	4	59	83	99	99
Heathwood Road north side				18	22	22	23
Tair Erw Road					28	28	28
Pedair Erw Road					25	25	25
Pum Erw Road					47	47	47
Llwynfedw Gardens					32	32	32
Ton-yr-ywen Avenue					37	104	104
Heol Dyfed							36
Heol Gwynedd							20
Heol Gwent							14
Heol Powis							68

Sources: Cardiff Directory; Electoral Registers. *Notes:* Figures for Caerphilly Road and Heathwood Road (north side, Birchgrove to Ton-yr-ywen Avenue are approximate only. The northern half of Ton-yr-ywen Avenue and the whole of Heol Dyfed, Heol Gwynedd, Heol Gwent and Heol Powis were developed after Ton-yr-ywen Farm was purchased by Cardiff Corporation. Heathwood Road was unnamed in 1909 and 1919.

a welcome feature of this well-planned street layout.

Work on Mountjoy's housing project at the lower end of the Ton-yr-ywen Estate had progressed as far north as Pum Erw Road when two events had a devastating impact on it. The first was the outbreak of war in September 1939, when house-building in general came to an immediate standstill, and the second was the Marquess of Bute's decision in the same year to part with his estates in Cardiff. Consequently, Mountjoy Ltd sold all its lands to Western Ground Rents Co. Ltd later in 1939, which meant that the driving force behind the private house-building venture on the Ton-yr-ywen Estate was removed when barely a third of the envisaged project had been completed. Within a few months all the undeveloped land north of Pum Erw Road had been turned over to allotment gardens.

In 1942 the British Oxygen Co. Ltd bought 15 acres of land between the present-day Powis Road and Maes-y-coed Road from Western Ground Rents to build a plant for the production of industrial gases. A small thatched cottage on the site was demolished in the 1930s. The factory was built opposite the middle of the three upper access gaps between the houses on Caerphilly Road but the company soon acquired a better entrance from Maes-y-coed Road after this was made up in 1946. During the war a part of the building was slightly damaged when a shell from a local battery accidentally fell on it. The plant was substantially extended after the war and remained fully operational until 1973 when half the site was sold to Bass Brewers Ltd for a distribution depot and regional office. BOC vacated the site completely in 1984 when the other half was sold to Bass. The whole of the property was acquired by S.A. Brain Ltd, the Cardiff brewer, in 1999.

At the end of the Second World War no attempt was made to revive Mountjoy's housing project, although 13 acres of land earmarked for building remained undeveloped between Pum Erw Road and the BOC plant. In an effort to alleviate the serious post-war accommodation shortage in Cardiff the council bought this land and built 206 on it in 1946–7. The Ton-yr-ywen brook was culverted and houses built on Ton-yr-ywen Avenue from Pum Erw Road to Maes-y-coed Road. Heol Dyfed was laid out from the middle access gap in Caerphilly Road and Heol Gwent, Heol Gwynedd and Heol Powis marked the completion of house-building on the Ton-yr-ywen Estate. These latest names commemorate the four ancient political divisions of Wales (see Table 5).

Return to Public Ownership

Cardiff Corporation began to cast covetous eyes on the Heath Estate during the opening decades of the twentieth century. Inspired, perhaps, by the high planning and building standards insisted upon by the Marquesses of Bute in all developments carried out on their extensive lands in Cardiff, the city pioneered an enlightened town planning scheme which their engineer, architect and surveyor proudly explained thus to members of the British Medical Association at their Cardiff meeting in 1928:

> The principal objects of such a scheme are to reserve the use of land for purposes which it is particularly suitable, to provide for laying out arterial and other main roads, to restrict the number of houses that may be erected on any one area (Cardiff had adopted a ratio of 8 houses per outer-zone acre) and to provide for ample open spaces (quantified by Cardiff at 10% of the total acreage to be developed)[1]

The most innovative, and perhaps contentious, of these four objectives was the council's recognition of the need to provide ample open spaces for recreational and leisure purposes in all future urban developments. Its great opportunity to implement these admirable guidelines came when the city absorbed 5,500 acres of surrounding countryside under the provisions of its 1922 boundary extension.

Heath House, with its attractive parkland, lay immediately north of Whitchurch Road in the parish of Llanishen, in an area within the city's newly acquired territory which had been earmarked for residential development. The park could be preserved as an ideal open space and become the focus for recreational and leisure use by the residents of the emerging northern suburbs. The corporation would have to act quickly, however, for the land of Allen's Bank Farm in the lower corner of the Heath Estate had already been built on and further housing projects were being planned for the remainder of the estate. Once building on the Heath had begun in earnest, the

---

[1] *The Book of Cardiff. Published to mark the B.M.A. visit* (1929).

32 The main front of Heath House, photographed in the 1930s.

price of land there would become too expensive to buy for mere recreational use.

Consequently, the council opened early negotiations for the purchase of Heath House and about 30 acres of its surrounding parkland. The caption above a photograph of the mansion in the *Western Mail* (22 April 1926) reads 'New Cardiff Recreation Ground', followed by an explanation that 'Cardiff Corporation are hopeful of securing Heath House, the residence of the late Mr Philip Turnbull, and its modern outbuildings and surrounding land, for public recreation purposes. Negotiations are proceeding with a view to their substitution for adjoining land already town-planned'. Turnbull had been a tenant at Heath House from 1917 until his death on 5 June 1925. He was a senior partner in the Cardiff shipowning firm of Turnbull Brothers which operated between 1877 and 1920. He was chairman of the Cardiff & Bristol Channel Shipowners' Association in 1895 and a justice of the peace for the county.[1] His son Paul lived on at Heath House until 1932. The Clark family had obviously made no agreement to sell either house or land during the 1920s and, following the departure of the Turnbull family, the tenancy was offered in 1932 to George Tucker, who became a well-known local entrepreneur.

Circumstances had changed by the late 1930s, however, when the corporation made a claim to purchase a wide strip of land across the Heath Estate in order to build Eastern Avenue, the second phase of its Northern Orbital Road, which it accompanied with a proposal 'to acquire the whole of the undeveloped portion of that part of the Heath Estate which lies between the Roath Branch line of the Great Western Railway

---

[1] Obituary in *St Peter's Magazine*, v (1925).

33 A Sunday school outing in the grounds of Heath House during the 1930s.

and Heathwood Road and which is bounded on the east by Allensbank Road and on the west by North Road and Caerphilly Road'.[1] It applied for grants and a government loan 'for the purchase of [the Heath Estate] for playing fields and other purposes' from the Local Area Committee set up under the powers of the Physical Training and Recreation Act, 1937, to enable it to implement its town planning scheme with ease in the city's rapidly developing northern suburbs.[2] The council had acquired Llandaff Court in 1931 in similar circumstances when it claimed land to build Western Avenue through the Insole Estate.

In January 1938 Wyndham Damer Clark agreed to sell Heath House and its remaining estate, except the land already built upon at Allen's Bank Farm and the Rhydhelig Avenue project, amounting to 203 acres, to the council for £105,000, which immediately set about allocating portions of its new acquisition to meet the objectives of its town planning scheme. There would be no shortage of claims for land, as the council would soon discover.

Its first act was to sell the north-eastern sector of the parkland surrounding Heath House to the Cardiff Education Committee for £10,383 for recreational use by secondary school pupils. In September 1939 this land was granted as playing fields for the specific use of Cathays High School. Still in 1939, the council decided to

[1] Cardiff Corporation, Estates Committee, 15 Dec. 1936.

[2] Estates Committee, 15 Sept. 1937.

designate the north-western corner of the Heath parkland as public playing fields under
the patronage of the National Playing Fields Association and obtained a £10,000 grant
from the King George V Memorial Fund to level and drain the ground and build a
pavilion on it.

A complication then arose: in September 1939 the War Office took possession of
Heath Park for military training and soon built lines of wooden hutments on the land
south of Heath House to accommodate troops. The council thus lost effective control
of its newly acquired property for, although part of the parkland was available as a
rule, it would often be declared out of bounds for undisclosed reasons.

When American troops were stationed at the camp towards the end of the war a
field behind Heath Park Avenue at the top end of the park was used as a 400-yard
landing strip for reconnaissance aircraft.[1] The park was released in 1946 although the
War Office refused to de-requisition the camp buildings until March 1951.

At the end of the war, the council revived its proposals for the Heath Estate. It
obtained an increased grant of £15,000 from the King George V Playing Fields
Association and by the end of 1946 had begun to landscape the parkland: 'Work on

34 The Heath Army Camp in 1942, almost engulfing the adjoining Heath House. The picture also shows
clearly the limit reached by pre-war house-building both in the Heath and, beyond the railway, Cyncoed.

[1] Reminiscences by Bob Davies in *Fly Past* (March 2000).

clearing unsightly trees, undergrowth, removing hedges and draining has been proceeding during the Autumn and Winter. Unfortunately, nothing can be done on the Camp Site or on developing the area used as arable land'.[1] The council decided to transfer all the playing fields and open spaces in the parkland to its Parks Committee. But, there were more surprises on the way.

The College of Education

In January 1946 the Ministry of Education informed the council that it wished to make immediate use of the army huts in the park as an Emergency Teachers' Training Centre for an estimated period of four years. This was agreed to and the wooden buildings were converted into study-bedrooms and a small hall, and facilities for athletics were provided. A high proportion of mature students, very many of them former members of the armed forces, were enrolled at the centre as part of the Ministry's effort to make up the shortfall of teachers in the country's classrooms as a result of the war.

35 One of the former Heath Army Camp huts occupied by the post-war Emergency Teachers' Centre, photographed in 1949.

[1] *Cardiff and Suburban News*, 22 Feb. 1947.

36 The former Heath Army Camp after its conversion into the City of Cardiff Training College.

The Emergency College functioned from 1946 to 1949 and proved such a success that when its term came to an end the City Education Committee decided to retain teacher training at the Heath site. It bought the buildings for £15,000, fenced off part of the parkland for track and field events, and opened its own Teachers' Training College there in September 1950, providing one-year supplementary courses for qualified teachers—physical education for men and art and crafts for both men and women. It had an academic staff of five, 26 students following the PE course, and 18 on the art and crafts course. The staff was enlarged to teach an extra nine subjects on the curriculum when two-year general training courses for men were added to its existing courses in 1956. These developments heralded a phase of rapid expansion and by 1960, when three-year courses were first taught, the number of students had risen to 208. Cardiff Training College had proved its merit and, in the winter of 1962, having outgrown its campus on the Heath, it moved to a spacious new site in Cyncoed. Two buildings on the original camp site are now used by the Heath Citizens Association but most of the site is occupied by the headquarters of the City's Sports and Leisure Department, which uses the former camp parade ground as its car-park. Meanwhile, the former College of Education has been amalgamated with other colleges in the city to become the University of Wales Institute, Cardiff.

Government Builings and Eastern Avenue

Following the Ministry of Education's claim, there came a request for a site on the Heath by yet another government department. During the aftermath of the war, Cardiff was rapidly developing as an administrative centre for Wales. Although the impressive offices of the Welsh Board of Health in Cathays Park (the nucleus of the later Welsh Office) had been opened in 1938, the Government was not yet ready to continue building on the land which it had bought directly behind it. Consequently, the Ministry of Works was obliged to find a suburban site which it could lease on reasonable terms. It made an application to build 'temporary buildings of light construction', similar to those it had already set up at Llanishen, on ten acres in the south-western corner of Heath Park, near Gabalfa.

It was no surprise when the Ministry of Transport added itself to the list of claimants for land on the Heath. Cardiff Corporation had built Western Avenue as far as Gabalfa in 1932 as part of its Northern Orbital Road project to divert through traffic away from the city centre. It had intended continuing the by-pass eastwards through the Heath Estate to rejoin the A48 trunk road at St Mellons, but this six-mile section of the scheme had to be deferred due to the outbreak of war and to land acquisition problems. The Roath Dock branch railway, running across the estate, was facing closure due to loss of traffic caused by the continuing decline of the coal trade at Cardiff Docks. It was therefore sensible to wait until this actually occurred and to buy the track from British Railways, so that Eastern Avenue could use the trackbed from Gabalfa to Penylan. An additional ribbon of land alongside the railway would also be needed to accommodate slip-roads and an updated dual carriageway wider than Western Avenue. It was not possible for the Ministry to approve this route until 1958, when a Preliminary Order was made, but funds were not made available until 1966. Work began in 1968 and Eastern Avenue was officially opened on 19 November 1971, at a final cost of £9.5m.

The council had not relinquished its pre-war commitments to release more parkland for private building. When the Estates Committee met in April 1947 it thought that it had made its final allocation of Heath Estate land thus: 28.3 acres for housing, 21.0 acres for education, 106.2 acres for parks and allotment gardens, and 58.8 acres for Eastern Avenue and temporary government buildings. Half the total acreage would remain as open ground (parkland and allotments) while the remainder would be let or sold for development (the teachers' training college, new government offices at Gabalfa, Eastern Avenue and housing). It proceeded to confirm these apportionments by implementing its decision to build a peripheral road, to be called King George V Drive, around the remaining open land of Heath Park and to lease land for private house-building along it. It also agreed to lease the 10 acres that the Ministry of Works needed to build its offices near Gabalfa from 1949 for a term of 42 years. The lease was assigned to the Department of the Environment on 21 March 1972.

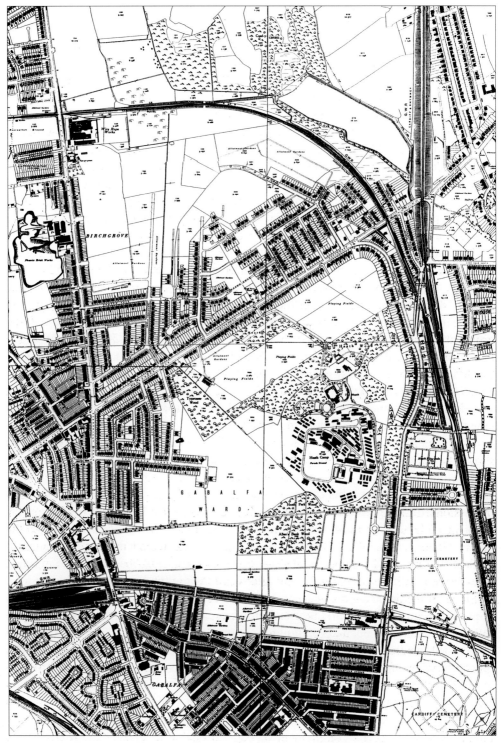

37 The Heath in 1947, showing the extent of development up to the Second World War.

The University Hospital of Wales

Late in 1949 it became known that the University of Wales Medical School, United Cardiff Hospitals, the Welsh Hospitals Board and Welsh Board of Health were still collectively pursuing their pre-war search for a site in Cardiff to erect a new teaching hospital and medical school. Five locations had been considered: at Culverhouse Cross, Leckwith, Lake Road East, Pontcanna Fields and Heath Park. The big surprise came when it was announced that the preferred site was Heath Park after the others had been discounted for a variety of reasons. When a formal request for a 53-acre site in the park was made to the council in February 1950 the issue immediately became contentious. Strong protests were voiced on behalf of 335 allotment holders who would be displaced by the proposal, by conservationists who opposed the destruction of so much mature woodland, and by others who deplored the inevitable loss of public amenity and constant urbanisation of the Heath Park environment.

The corporation was divided over the matter, as the conflicting recommendations made by its committees reveal. At a council meeting early in March 1950, J.H. Morgan, who led the opposition to granting the site, reminded members that 'the Heath Estate was purchased under the Physical Recreation Act for a specific purpose, to be retained as a recreation area for the whole of the city'. Supporters of the proposal, however, insisted that, of the five locations considered, Heath Park was the most appropriate one, bearing in mind its closeness to the centre of population in Cardiff and also its ease of access to the developing pattern of main roads making contact with the remainder of South Wales. They also warned that, if the Heath site was denied to the medical authorities, they would be forced to build the prestigious new hospital at a location outside the city boundary.

The latter was a compelling argument. It was more than justifiable that the hospital should be sited in Cardiff simply because its establishment was the natural outcome of developments which had been taking place for a long time within the city. Ever since 1893, intending doctors had been able to undertake the pre-clinical phase of their professional training in the medical sciences department of University College. By 1921 the college, in conjunction with the Cardiff Royal Infirmary, had established the Welsh National School of Medicine in Newport Road which provided a course of clinical training for its students. This was a big step forward because doctors could receive their entire professional training at Cardiff from that year onward.

Since all medical schools were obliged to have access to hospital patients in order to provide their students with essential first-hand experience it was arranged that the Infirmary should make a minimum number of beds available for training activities by the Cardiff Medical School. As the new medical school grew, so did its need for a greater number of beds and, before long, other local hospitals were also called upon to provide the necessary minimum number. By the late 1930s, however, the demand for beds was again threatening to outstrip supply and drastic action was needed to safeguard this vital provision. Urgent plans were made to extend the Infirmary buildings to increase its complement of beds to enable it to meet the needs of the medical school and those of the expanding medical services of the era. But it soon became apparent that the Infirmary site was too small and traffic problems were making access to it increasingly difficult. The only alternative was to build a large new hospital somewhere on the outskirts of Cardiff to overcome the problems which were threatening the future of health care and medical training in the city. The search for a site was interrupted by the Second World War but, by 1949, the medical authorities were adamant that Heath Park was the only remaining site within the city which was acceptable to them. Cardiff councillors made their final assessment of the situation in March 1950 and decided, by 32 votes to 18, to offer the Heath Park site to the medical authorities for their new hospital.[1] The land was sold to the Ministry of Health on 31 March 1952.

From the outset it was recognised that, because medical science was constantly developing, needs would change as time progressed. Consequently, plans for the new hospital would have to allow for the maximum amount of internal adaptation to the building without changing its main structure. It was felt that a competition would be the best way to attract architects with sufficient experience to satisfy this requirement. The competition, which attracted over 300 entrants, was held in 1961 and the winning entry was accepted. In recognition of the pressing need for dentists in Wales at that time work on the Dental School was begun in 1963 and it was ready to accept its first students in 1965. The school was officially opened the following year. The main building phase also began in 1966 with the construction of the Medical Teaching Centre with 800 beds, which was opened on 19 November 1971 at a total cost of £20m. Today, the University Hospital of Wales has become one of the greatest focuses of activity within the whole city.

During the 1980s sporadic house-building projects were undertaken at a number of infill locations on the Heath, at Heath Mead, Heath Park Drive and Eton Court. In 1991 the All Nations Centre, with access from Sachville Avenue, was opened on an elongated triangle of land between the Heath allotment gardens and Eastern Avenue. It was established by the Covenant Life Church, an international movement which promotes evangelism, community work and Third World relief aid. Major building activity in the area has, hopefully, now come to an end. In the spring of 1996 positive action was taken to conserve the 23 surviving acres of local woodland with the founding of the Friends of Heath Park Woodland, a group of volunteers who work in cooperation with the park rangers to plant and manage trees and shrubs, protect plants and animals in their natural habitat, repair footpaths and undertake maintenance.

[1] *Cardiff Times*, 11 March 1950.

The Second World War and Afterwards

House-building on the Heath Estate during the First World War had been severely curtailed. The Second World War caused even wider disruption because the scale of building activity there had increased so dramatically by 1939, when all housing projects came to an abrupt end for about ten years. Some were revived at the end of that period, others had to be adapted to meet changed circumstances, while the remainder had to be abandoned completely.

Air Raids on the Heath

The reality of the war was brought home early to the Heath. An associated company of a German engineering firm called the Flottmann Drill Company had bought a factory off Allensbank Road on a site alongside the Roath Dock railway. During the 1930s Hans Kuenemann had come from Germany to manage this factory and it is alleged that he was a German spy. Apparently, he had narrowly managed to escape home at the outbreak of war taking with him information that would help the Luftwaffe plan their persistent air attacks on Cardiff between 1940 and 1944. Their main objective, undoubtedly, was the docks but other strategic locations were also targetted. The Royal Ordnance Factory in the angle of Caerphilly Road and Tŷ Glas Road would probably have been one of them and Heath Camp another, although neither was hit by bombs. The only loss of life at the Ordnance Factory occurred when a shell fired from a local anti-aircraft gun accidentally fell through the roof and exploded inside the building.

Many residential areas of Cardiff suffered bomb damage, especially those in the vicinity of the docks. Some of these incidents can only be interpreted as deliberate acts of revenge or as attempts to undermine civilian morale, especially as some were caused by landmines. The effect of their explosions was so powerful that, in order to allow time for the aeroplane that dropped them to get clear, they were released attached to a parachute. This meant that they could not be aimed accurately, for they would drift down with the wind and land quite indiscriminately. One had fallen at the corner of St Tanwg Road and St Edwen Gardens on ground earmarked for building but had, fortunately, been abandoned at the beginning of the war. The blast caused severe damage to nearby houses, however. Another descended on the garden of 35 St Agnes Road on a moonlit night on 18 May 1943, totally destroying the house, along with a number of others, and causing many casualties, including nine deaths. The occupants of the house were Ivor Williams, his wife Edith May, and their 22-year-old daughter Megan. Mr Williams was then the secretary of the Cardiff branch of Y Cymmrodorion, the Welsh cultural and literary society. All three died. Inside the cover of the branch minute book for the years 1926–53 is the following stark inscription: 'Civil Defence Rescue Service: Recovered from St Agnes Road, 21/5/43'. The book had obviously been found in the rubble of the house and returned to the society. As a tribute to Ivor Williams and his family the next branch secretary added a statement about the tragedy to the book.

A commemorative feature in the *South Wales Echo* (27 May 1993), written fifty years after the event, gives a graphic account of the devastation in St Agnes Road. More recently, Mrs Margaret James, now resident in King George V Drive, has provided personal recollections of this horrific episode. At that time she was a child living in one of the houses which were destroyed and had recently celebrated her sixth birthday:

> My parents, my eight-year-old brother, Ronald, my six-week-old sister, Valerie, and I managed to survive by being in a Morrison shelter in the kitchen. When the dust had settled my father said that we would have to get out before the house collapsed. He carried me, my mother carried Valerie and Ron had to walk out barefoot over the glass on the floor. Our house was only just being held up by the staircase. When we got out, all we could see of the other houses was rubble. At the same time, our neighbours managed to get out of their house. I especially remember seeing their canary, which they had brought out with them in its cage, still alive but with its feathers blown off. Later, my mother took us on the tram, wearing raincoats over our pyjamas, to relatives who were able to house us for a while.[1]

The Revd Herbert White, who was a pupil at Birchgrove School at that time, recollected the incident many years later:

> Many mornings going to school we picked up shrapnel; fragments of shells, bombs or landmines that showered down in the Blitz. On some days we had to make detours about holes blown in the road. Sometimes bombs had fallen on houses along our route (down Caerphilly Road). A whole road on the Heath had a direct hit from a land mine.[2]

John Vodden remembers the school's air raid precautions:

> There were three air raid shelters, one in each of the playgrounds, but this did not provide sufficient room for all the pupils. Those who lived within a couple of minutes walk, or run, of the school were required to go home in the event of an air raid during school time. To ensure this evacuation was carried out in an orderly manner with due regard for road safety,

[1] From a conversation with the author.

[2] This and the following quotations are from *Birchgrove Primary School Centenary* (1997).

these pupils were divided into four teams, each of which was provided with a different coloured band: red, blue, yellow or green. At the sound of the siren one team would assemble at the school gates and be directed by the teachers to the Birchgrove Inn and then northwards up Caerphilly Road, a second team would be marshalled at the Birch. and then sent eastwards along Heathwood Road while a third team would be dispatched southwards from the same point. The fourth team was directed westwards along Philog Road (later called Birchgrove Road). There would be few members of this last team because the school lay practically on the north west boundary of the city at that time.

Birchgrove School's log book gives additional information:

4th Sept. 1940: Air raid alarm 9.40. Those present went to shelter. All-clear went at 10.05 but we saw a fight going on above and sheltered for ten minutes more. Then we resumed work. Second alarm this morning 10.25. Children dispersed. All-clear 10.40. School resumed work.

Air raid warnings also occurred on 12, 17 (twice), 18, 25, 26 and 27 (twice) September, 16, 21 (twice) and 28 October, 11 and 21 November and 11 December 1940. On 6 January 1941 the headteacher noted: 'School resumed work four days after the Cardiff "Blitz". This area has not suffered much—only the top of Caerphilly Road'.

Other areas in Cardiff were not so lucky, especially those in the south of the city. Families who had suffered the trauma of being bombed out of their homes were re-housed by the council in a number of Shelter Colonies on the fringe of the city. One of these was built on former Bute land near the old brickworks pond at the top end of Crystal Glen. In the spring of 1945 the corporation demolished these shelters, replaced them with about 140 prefabricated bungalows and named this temporary layout 'The Crystals', due to its location by the Crystal Wood. In 1947 Roman Catholic members of this community began to worship in the simple welfare centre which had been provided by the council. At this time, as the centre was used for dancing on Saturday evenings, preparations for Mass could not take place until after 11.00 p.m. and, immediately after the Mass, the altar had to be removed so that the hall could be used by other denominations. Membership increased and by 1952 a lease was taken out on the welfare centre, which was transformed into a church hall serving the new Roman Catholic parish of Heath and Llanishen created as a result of this arrangement. In 1964, worshippers moved to the modern parish church dedicated to St Brigid slightly to the north of the old hall.[1]

---

[1] *Saint Brigid's Church* (1964).

38 An aerial view of the Crystals, to the north of Heathwood Road, dating from the 1940s, showing temporary housing built for families made homeless by bombing.

Americans and Squatters

In the early years of the war, Heath Camp was used for regular training purposes. Later, it became a base for American troops as part of the gigantic preparations being made for the invasion of France. Local people remember large numbers of Army vehicles that were awaiting shipment from the docks being parked for cover under the trees in Heath Park at that time.

Also early in the war the Heath Householders Society was set up to provide entertainment for the troops at Heath Camp. On 27 June 1942 they held a Country Fair at Tucker's Field, Heath House, as one the means they used to maintain the funds they needed to finance the concerts, socials and other events they provided for the soldiers.[1]

The following reminiscences give an insight into one of these concerts and also the stringent living conditions endured towards the end of the war:

[1] See the *Cardiff and Suburban News*, 20 June 1942.

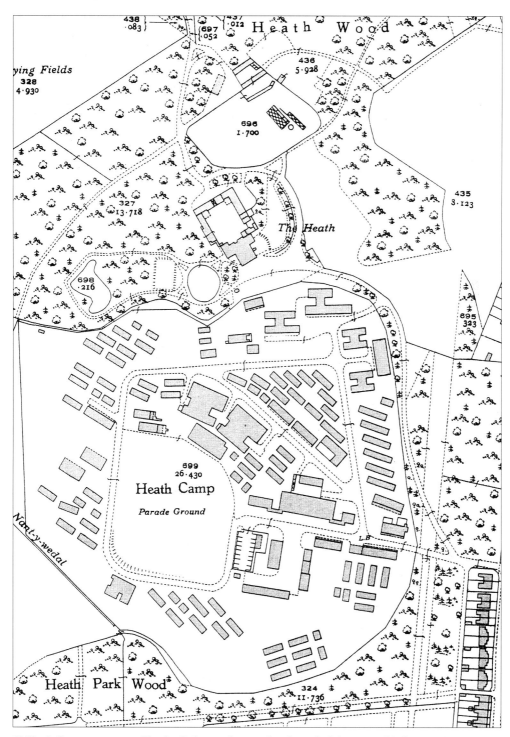

39 Heath Camp, as portrayed by the Ordnance Survey after the end of the war and before Heath House was demolished.

We had joined St Joseph's Youth Club and its Concert Party. Naturals for the Concert Party and revelling in its glamour, we performed in Panto-mimes, Plays, Musicals and Concerts ... The Yanks had not yet departed our shores. Rationing was still in force and we went to take a Concert up to the Heath Camp, an American camp at the top of Allensbank Road. On the night we gave a superb performance. Back-stage, people were changing, packing scenery, etc., when an official of the camp called us all to order and invited us, when ready, to refresh ourselves at the buffet provided in the next tent along. All reminders, threats and warnings were as nothing faced with a top-heavy mound of extravagance that was the buffet. It displayed as decoration items not seen in six years of war. We pigged out on ham and pineapples, pies bursting with real meat, beer from a can, cheeses and fresh boiled eggs. It was all here, a ten minute walk from home. Bellies full, we set to, filling pockets, bags, umbrellas and knicker legs. Who knew when, if ever, we would have such a chance again.[1]

The camp on the Heath was soon to be vacated by the Americans, although it was not to be de-requisitioned by the War Office for some time. Due to the abandonment of house-building during the war years and the destruction caused by air raids there was an acute shortage of accommodation in Cardiff during the immediate post-war period. One temporary solution adopted by local authorities was to allow needy families to occupy camps and billets as they were gradually vacated by the armed forces. This occurred at the Heath where a sector of the camp was made available for occupation. Tina Fraser again recalls:

Housing at this time was a desperate situation. Thousands of houses were destroyed in the War along with our skilled workmen. For young married people with small families things were tough, many formed Squatters' Clubs with committees and working officials, securing rights to vacated camps and buildings previously occupied by the forces. The first we knew that the Yanks were on the move was a visit from Uncle Gwyn. The Americans were vacating Heath Camp and he wanted the family to support their attempt to squat on the day. On the dawn of that day, the would-be squatters faced the main gate. Close-packed and enclosed in a barrier of friends and relatives preventing non-squatters' club intruders getting through. Each young family clutched to them a hut number and directions to it within the camp provided the night before by well-informed club organisers. At the very instant the last lorry thundered past, the squatters were through the gate and running, friends and family

---

[1] Tina M. Fraser, *City of Trees* (1993).

bringing up the rear. Once in, it would take another army to get them out. Time saw curtains and bright paint transform the camp-site into a village, flower and vegetable gardens filled the spaces between makeshift homes. Other areas were formed into parks and playgrounds for many post-war babies now grown to play.[1]

As civilian life returned to normal the camp community at the Heath gradually dwindled, then faded away, as private building and local authority housing began to meet needs.

Heath Citizens' Assocation

It has been suggested that the events that occurred at the camp for a brief period during 1940 had an important influence upon the decision made to set up the Heath Citizens' Association in 1946. This organisation was to become a highly significant motivator which strengthened and enriched the lives of local residents for a whole generation. The events occured in the immediate aftermath of the evacuation of the British Expeditionary Force from France in the early summer of 1940, when a group of soldiers who had survived the horrors of Dunkirk were given temporary refuge at Heath Camp. They had been traumatised and were in sore need of a prolonged period of rehabilitation. They were deeply appreciative of the welcome and support extended to them by local residents during their stay at the Heath and acknowledged how critical a part this played in their eventual recovery.

This same spirit of friendship had also served to bond members of ARP Post 225 which was responsible for countering the effects of enemy air raids in the area around Allensbank Road and Heath Park Avenue. These were local residents who realised that their sense of brotherhood had been a deep source of strength to them as they went about their dangerous work during the war and they wished to extend its benefits into the post-war era. This excerpt from the Chairman's Message in the HCA Handbook for 1949–50 provides a clear statement of purpose:

> During the war years a community spirit was born and developed through adversity and danger. Worldly possessions or station in life did not matter when the sirens sounded. The hardships experienced created a bond of friendship and good fellowship. We in the Heath were saved the horrors experienced in other parts of our City, yet we remember how neighbours welcomed us to share their shelters and their company.
>
> Most of us felt that the good spirit that prevailed in A.R.P. Post 225 was the essence of good living and should be maintained.

[1] Ibid.

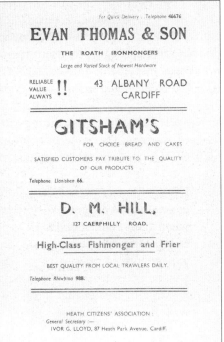

40 The programme for the Heath Citizens' Association summer fair in 1952. Both the promised events and the advertisements are redolent of a vanished age.

A public meeting was held at Rhyd-y-pennau School in 1946 in order to seek support for setting up a local organisation with the prime function of promoting 'good fellowship, good citizenship and good neighbourliness'. The suggestion was taken up enthusiastically with the immediate election of officers along with wardens to represent six sectors within the membership area. They were Allensbank Road (north), Heathwood Grove, Highfield Road, Heath Park Avenue, Heath Park Crescent and Crystal Avenue.

The HCA Handbook for 1949–50 shows that, within a few years of its founding, the association had already built up a membership of 400 and had created a vigorous programme of summer and winter activities which were held mainly in the Teachers' Training Centre on the Heath. During the winter session, meetings were held each evening of the week, every week. On Monday there was a youth club, on Tuesday arts and crafts, on Wednesday educational classes, on Thursday drama and arts and crafts, on Friday woodwork and metalwork, and on Saturday drama again. A notice in the 1949 winter programme speaks volumes:

> A number of Chess-players have expressed their interest in the formation of a Club, but difficulty has been experienced in the arrangement of a Club Night owing to the number of activities in connection with the

41 The marriage of George Tucker's daughter in the late 1940s, with the party photographed in front of the main entrance to Heath House.

42 Heath House towards the end of its time as the headquarters of the Heath Citizens' Association.

> Association which have a claim on the time of the members. Suggestions
> would be welcomed …

A social committee was responsible for arranging occasional whist drives, socials, children's parties and other events. The summer programme consisted of bowls matches, an annual Countrie Fayre at Heath Park and coach trips to beauty spots and places of interest. 'In arranging these excursions the committee endeavour to provide educational value in addition to social enjoyment', said the association handbook. A comment from the account of an excursion to Cheltenham in the summer of 1948 suggests that the association was already thinking about setting up its own centre on the Heath at that time. The Ministry of Education was due to give up its lease on the Teachers' Training Centre the following year and the future of the former Army camp buildings was unsure. 'On the way to Cheltenham we called at Llanvair Discoed, near Caerwent, and there viewed a recreational centre which many felt was of the type we needed in Heath Park'.[1]

Early in 1949 Heath House was vacated by George Tucker, who had occupied it since 1932, during the final years of the Clark family's ownership of the estate. He

---

[1] *Heath Citizens' Association Handbook* (1949–50).

was a highly energetic entrepreneur who established and maintained a number of successful local businesses. Before and during the Second World War, with the aid of his family, he worked three farms, ran a garage at 184 Caerphilly Road, and had a mortar-mill at a yard near Heath Halt (High). His most notable achievement was Tucker's Transport Company, a haulage concern which he ran from the courtyard of Heath House itself; his fleet of lorries was among the first to be nationalised in January 1949. Following Tucker's departure, the HCA had obviously made an application to use Heath House as its centre because, on 21 November 1950, Cardiff Parks Committee agreed to the following proposal: 'Heath House Community Centre (run by the Joint Adult Education Committee) propose to allow Heath Citizens' Association the use of Heath House on condition that the Association is prepared to widen its membership to include residents from the whole (Heath) area'.

The HCA thus gained a prestigious mansion house as its headquarters and, as a result of the terms included in the agreement, this remarkably energetic and imaginative association came to extend its activities throughout the whole Heath suburb during the 1950s. It used Heath House as a centre for over thirteen years and the resulting stability gave it an opportunity to consolidate its existing activities and take up new ones, including an annual eisteddfod, first held at Ton-yr-ywen School in May 1954, which attracted a wide circle of regular participants and followers.

Nowadays, the objectives which inspired the association's sense of vision during the immediate post-war period are being undermined by powerful modern trends, not least the relentless competition for people's leisure-time activities, often spurred on by a commercially motivated entertainment industry. The HCA's 'Five Objectives' are printed prominently in their 1949–50 Handbook and include, first and foremost: 'To promote good fellowship and neighbourliness'. What a healthy role model for an emerging Neighbourhood Watch initiative!

This account ends on a sombre note. In 1964 the HCA was forced to move its headquarters back to its original premises due to the structural deterioration of Heath House. Rainwater percolating through the flat roof caused persistent problems. It was allowed to use one of the buildings which had been vacated by staff and students of the former teachers' training college nearby, following their move to a new campus in Cyncoed. Heath House was left empty. The following appeared in the *South Wales Echo* (30 November 1965):

Mystery fire at 3.30 a.m. destroys Heath House

Firemen were today damping down the embers of a mystery fire which gutted Heath House, the former Headquarters of the Heath Citizens' Association, at Heath Park, Cardiff. The alarm was given at 3.30 a.m. today and by the time firemen had arrived the whole building was ablaze. They brought the fire under control by 5.00 a.m. but not before the roof and interior had been destroyed.

43 George Tucker surveys the burnt-out remains of his former home as it is demolished in 1966.

Within a few months the building was demolished because its condition was causing danger to the public. George Tucker, the last person to live in the mansion, had this to say as the house was pulled down on 29 April 1966: 'It is a terrible thing to see it die. At one time it was alive with activity but now the house and all it meant to everyone is in bits. It had the finest situation and atmosphere of any house in the city but now it has all gone. It is very sad'.[1]

[1] *Western Mail*, 29 April 1966.

Sources Consulted

The Heath: A Short Guide

Records of the Royal Commission on the Ancient and Historical Monuments of Wales (Aberystwyth).
Cardiff Records (ed. J.H. Matthews), vol. ii (1900), vol. iii (1901).
A.A. Pettigrew, *Cardiff Parks*, vol. i (1926).
John Roland Phillips, *The Civil War in Wales and the Marches* (1878).
S.K. Binny, *History of St Mark's, Gabalfa* (1976).
Bute Estate Map, *c.* 1770–80 (National Library of Wales).
A book of maps of the Estates of Thomas Edwards (1776) by E. Thomas (National Library of Wales).
Russel Gascoigne, *The Haunting of Glamorgan and Gwent* (1993).
Records of the Great Sessions in Wales (National Library of Wales).
Deirdre Beddoe, *Welsh Convict Women* (1979).
M. Lowder, *The Confessions and Behaviour of Henry James and Catharine Griffiths* (1791) (Cardiff Central Library).
Roger L. Brown (ed.), *Turn of the Century Ton* (1982).
Cardiff Corporation. Reports of Council and Committees (Cardiff Central Library).
Edgar L. Chappell, 'Notes on Cardiff: Heaths' (1940) (Cardiff Central Library).
Edgar L. Chappell, 'Cuttings, plans and pamphlets re Cardiff (1900–47)' (Cardiff Central Library).

Axe and Arrow

National Museum of Wales.
Royal Commission on the Ancient and Historical Monuments of Wales.
Glamorgan-Gwent Archaeological Trust.
W.F. Grimes, *The Prehistory of Wales* (1951).
Illustrated Dictionary of Archaeology (1977).
Chris Musson, *Wales from the Air* (1994).
H.N. Savory, 'The Early Bronze Age in Glamorgan' in *Glamorgan County History*, ii (1984).

Ffynnon Llandenis

Royal Commission on the Ancient and Historical Monuments of Wales.
Glamorgan-Gwent Archaeological Trust.
S. Baring-Gould and J. Fisher, *The Lives of the British Saints* (1907–13).
Francis Jones, *The Holy Wells of Wales* (1954).
Cardiff Records. (ed. J.H. Matthews), v (1905).
N. Carlisle, *Topographical Dictionary of Wales* (1811).
M. Trevelyan, *Folk Lore and Folk Stories of Wales* (1909).
T. Breveton, *The Book of Welsh Saints* (2000).
John Hilling, 'Cardiff', in *South Glamorgan. A County History* (ed. Stewart Williams) (1975).
Eirlys Gruffydd, *Ysbrydion Gwent a Morgannwg* (1998).

Battle of the Great Heath

G.J. Williams, *Traddodiad Llenyddol Morgannwg* (1948).
Rice Merrick, *Morganiae Archaiographia* (ed. by Brian Ll. James) (1983).
Ralph Griffiths, 'The Twelve Knights of Glamorgan', *Glamorgan Historian* (ed. Stewart Williams), iii (1967).

G.T. Clark, *Limbus Patrum Morganiae et Glamorganiae* (1896).
Thomas Nicholas, *The History and Antiquities of Glamorgan* (1874).
Cardiff Records (ed. J.H. Matthews), vols. i, ii, iv (1898–1903).
Aneirin Talfan Davies, *Crwydro Bro Morgannwg*, i (1972).

Racing on the Heath

William Rees, *Cardiff. A History of the City* (1969).
Dennis Morgan, *The Cardiff Story* (1991).
A.A. Pettigrew, *Cardiff Parks*, i (1926).
Cardiff Records (ed. J.H. Matthews), iv (1903).
John Davies, *Cardiff and the Marquesses of Bute* (1981).
Leonard Dowse, *Llanishen and Lisvane* (1972).

Enclosure of the Heath

William Rees, *Cardiff. A History of the City* (1969).
The Diaries of John Bird, 1790–1803 (ed. Hilary M. Thomas) (1987).
Cardiff Records (ed. J.H. Matthews), ii, iii, iv (1900–03).
Heath Inclosure Award (1803) (Glamorgan Record Office).
Minutes of Cardiff District Turnpike Trust (Glamorgan Record Office).
Llanishen Parish Vestry Books (Glamorgan Record Office).
Edgar L. Chappell, 'Notes on Cardiff: Heaths' (1940) (Cardiff Central Library).
Edgar L. Chappell, 'Notes on Cardiff Turnpike Trust' (Cardiff Central Library).

The Lewis Family

A.H. Williams, *An Introduction to the History of Wales* (1948).
Fred, Vida and John Holley, *Master of Hounds* (1987).
Edgar L. Chappell, *Old Whitchurch* (1945).
Will of the Revd W.P. Lewis (Glamorgan Record Office).
Map of Race Course land sold to Wyndham W. Williams by Cardiff Corporation (1849) by G.S. Strawson (Glamorgan Record Office).
Papers of the Wyndham Lewis (Murray-Threipland) of New House, Llanishen, Estate (Glamorgan Record Office).
The Cambrian.
Cardiff Times.
Cardiff and Merthyr Guardian.
The Field.

The Bute Brickworks

John Davies, *Cardiff and the Marquesses of Bute* (1981).
Survey of the Marquess of Bute's Estates by David Stewart (1824) (Glamorgan Record Office).
Cardiff: an illustrated handbook (ed. John Ballinger) (1886).
Cardiff Argus, 5 July 1890.
A map of all Llanishen Estate by William Morrice (1777) (National Library of Wales).
Minutes of Llanishen Parish Council, 1894–1911 (Glamorgan Record Office).
Minutes of Cardiff Corporation Parliamentary Committee, 21 Dec. 1896 (Cardiff Central Library).
Census enumerators' books (microfilm, Glamorgan Record Office and Cardiff Central Library).

Two Railways

G.A. Sekon, 'Cardiff: the city, its railways and commerce', *Railway Magazine*, xx (1907).
D.S. Barrie, *The Rhymney Railway* (1952).
R.W. Kidner, *The Rhymney Railway* (1995).
S. Richards, *The Cardiff Railway* (1977).
Eric R. Mountford, *The Cardiff Railway* (1987).
Chris W. James, 'The Coryton Line', *Treoda*, 6 Dec. 1965, and 7 March 1976.
Brian J. Miller, *South Wales Railways at the Grouping* (1986).
H. Morgan, *South Wales Branch Lines* (1984).
John Davies, *Cardiff and the Marquesses of Bute* (1981).
Philip Riden and Keith Edwards, *Families and Farms in Lisvane* (1993).
R.A. Cooke, *Atlas of the Great Western Railway, as at 1947* (1988).

Urbanisation

A.K. Hignell, 'Suburban development in North Cardiff, 1850–1919: a case study of the patterns and processes of growth in the parishes of Llanishen, Lisvane and Whitchurch' (Unpublished Ph.D. thesis, University of Wales (Cardiff), 1987).
M.J. Daunton, *Coal Metropolis. Cardiff 1870-1914* (1977).
William Rees, *Cardiff. A History of the City* (1969).
Cardiff 1889-1974. The Story of the County Borough (1974).
Dennis Morgan, *The Cardiff Story* (1991).
John Davies, *Cardiff and the Marquesses of Bute* (1981).
G.T. Clark, *Limbus Patrum Morganiae et Glamorganiae* (1896).
P. Moore, 'Cardiff slums of 1849', *Glamorgan Historian*, ii (1965).
Thomas Bowen, *Dinas Caerdydd a'i Methodistiaeth Galfinaidd* (1927).
John Williamson (ed.), *History of Congregationalism in Cardiff and District* (1920).
Cardiff Directories, various issues.
Cardiff. Reports of Council and Committees (Cardiff Central Library).
Will of the Revd W. Price Lewis, 1848 (Glamorgan Record Office).
Papers of the Wyndham Lewis (Murray-Threipland) of New House, Llanishen, Estate (Glamorgan Record Office).
Reports by Head Officers of Cardiff City Council on the proposed extension of the City Area, 1910 (Cardiff Central Library).
Electoral Registers (Cardiff Central Library).
Census enumerators' books (microfilm, Glamorgan Record Office and Cardiff Central Library).
The Cardiff Spectator, ii, nos. 10 and 11 (1961).
Industrial Wales, no. 4 (June 1948).
Western Mail, 1 October 1984 (advertising feature).
Telephone Directories, 1947–97 (Cardiff Central Library).
Medical Officer of Health, Cardiff. Annual Report (1926).
District Land Registry for Wales.

Return to Public Ownership

Cardiff County Council, Heath Estate Papers.
Cardiff 1889–1974. The story of the County Borough (1974).
John Newman, *The Buildings of Wales. Glamorgan* (1995).
The Book of Cardiff. Published to mark the British Medical Association's 96th Annual Meeting held in Cardiff (1928).
Cardiff. Reports of Council and Committees (Cardiff Central Library).
Official Opening of Cyncoed Teachers' Training College, 1963–64 Academic Year. Commemorative Programme (University of Wales Institute, Cardiff).

Arnold S. Aldis, *Cardiff Royal Infirmary 1883–1983* (1984).
John Surtees and Alan Trevor Jones, 'The Medical Teaching Centre Cardiff', *Western Mail*, supplement,
    19 Nov. 1971.
Cardiff and Suburban News, 22 Feb. 1947.

The Second World War and Afterwards

Dennis Morgan, *The Cardiff Story* (1991).
Dennis Morgan, *Cardiff. A City at War* (1998).
J.H. Morgan, 'Cardiff at War' in *The Cardiff Book* (ed. Stewart Williams) (1977).
Tina M. Fraser, *City of Trees* (1993).
Birchgrove Primary School Centenary (The School, 1997).
Saint Brigid's Church (1964).
Handbook 1949–1950 (Heath Citizens' Association, Cardiff).
Cardiff Corporation. Reports of Council and Committees (Cardiff Central Library).
South Wales Echo.
Western Mail.
Cardiff and Suburban News, 20 June 1942.

Index

As far as possible, places within the borough of Cardiff as it existed before 1875 have been indexed under Cardiff; other places within the modern city, including streets and buildings in the Heath, have been indexed separately. Except where indicated, all place-names are in Glamorgan.